TALES
— OF —
TRAUMA

A journey through stories of
abuse in the Scriptures

WALTER FIRTH

A PSALM OF DAVID

O God of my praise: do not keep silent;
The wicked and the deceitful open
their mouths against me;
They speak against me with lying tongues.
They encircle me with words of hatred;
and fought against me without cause.
They answer my love with false
accusation: but I turned to prayer.
They repay me evil for good,
and hatred for my love.

Let a wicked man be appointed over him;
let an accuser stand at his right side;
Let he be judged and found guilty;
let his prayer become sin.
Let his days be few; may another
take over his office.
Let his children be orphans,
his wife a widow.
Let his children be cast out of
their habitations and wander
without a dwelling-place,
Let them beg in search of bread
from their desolate places.
Let his creditor seize all his possessions;
and strangers plunder his labour.
Let there be no one to show him mercy;
and let no one pity his fatherless children;
Let his children be given up to utter
destruction; their names blotted
out in the next generation.
Let Yahweh remember the iniquity
of his fathers; let not the sin of
his mother be blotted out.
Let Yahweh be continually aware
of them and cause their names
to be cut off from the earth.
Because he was not minded to act
kindly, but persecuted the poor and
needy man, that he might even slay
one crushed and broken in spirit.

As he loved to curse—let a
curse come upon him!
As he did not delight in blessing—
let blessing be far from him!
Let him be clothed in a curse like a garment:
Let it come as water into his bowels,
and as oil into his bones.
Let it be like the cloak he wraps around
him, and like the belt he continually wears.
Let this be how Yahweh repays my accusers:
and all those who speak evil against me.

But you, Lord Yahweh, deal
mercifully with me, as befits your
name: for your mercy is good.
Deliver me, for I am poor and needy;
and my heart is pierced within me.
I am fading away like a lengthening
shadow: I am shaken off like locusts.
My knees are weakened from fasting, and
my flesh is lean, and has lost its fat.
To my accusers I have become the
object of their scorn; when they
see me, they shake their head.
Help me, Yahweh, my God; and save
me according to your kindness.
Let them know that it is your hand;
that you, Yahweh, have done it.
Let them curse, but you bless;
When they rise up, they will be put to
shame while your servant rejoices.

My accusers shall be clothed in shame:
wrapped in their disgrace as in a robe.
With my mouth I will sing to
Yahweh in abundance;
That my delight in Yahweh may
shine in the midst of many:
For Yahweh stands at the right
hand of the needy;
To save him from those who
would condemn his soul.

CONTENTS

The Purpose of this Study 1
Creation 3
Murder 15
The Wife and the Handmaid 22
Sodom 33
Violation & Vengeance 42
The Daughter-in-Law 52
The Warrior's Vow 61
The Levite's Concubine 70
The Daughter of a King 83
The Little Children and the She Bears 91
Cannibal 96
War 104

THE PURPOSE OF THIS STUDY

As Human beings, we exist in a world constructed by a library of narratives. All meaning and understanding are subjective truths. Even objective truth: confirmed by science and universally accepted, is only relative; it is only realistic based on time, the place, and the circumstances that people find themselves in. As such, the truths of the world an individual and community have are built into their lived schemas by the stories they hold to be true. Each of the twelve stories here are not stories about how things should be: they are the opposite. Each story describes how things were and how things should not be. In a world where abuse and trauma are ever present, yet frequently silenced, knowing the stories of our past gives us a language and understanding by which we can better engage more safely, more supportively, and more humanely, as a community than we have previously. This will enable us to build a new narrative, new truths, and a new, kinder future.

GETTING STARTED

The stories in this study are built out of stories that make up the Old Testament. Oft-times there are legends, stories, oral traditions and background information that did not necessarily make it into the stories as we read them today. Sometimes in the Scriptures we later find terms, additional detail or responses that are no longer part of the story as it has been recorded. For ease and narrative purposes, such information has been re-applied to the stories as they are told here.

In order for us to sit in the stories, they have also been written in such a way that narrative can flow. If you are after a literal translation, I suggest that you consult your own Bible translations.

We should not be afraid to engage in the stories that our faith has built up or been built around. Sadly, this also means that there are encounters and interactions between and amongst God's people that are painful, cruel, and abusive. Frequently we skim over, or out rightly ignore, such stories. The stories in this study have been written in such a way that we can be confronted with the brutality and shadow-side of our human nature and hopefully come to a deeper realization about how to be God's people, how to engage and sit within stories of trauma and abuse in our lives and communities, and I hope, how to live lives that are kinder and more graceful than those that have come before us.

CREATION

I, the teller of this story, proclaim God's glorious splendour so as to frighten and terrify all the spirits of the destroying angels, the spirits of illegitimacy, demons, Lilith, howlers, and desert dwellers. I tell this story to frighten and to terrify spirits such as those which fall upon men without warning with the aim of leading them astray from a spirit of understanding and to make their heart and their soul desolate during this present dominion of wickedness and predetermined time of humiliations for the children of light. And I tell this story to you, my listener, in order that your understanding of creation may be deepened on your journey to find truth.

In the days when Yahweh made the earth and the heavens, He split open and divided the sea by His powerful strength and broke the heads of the dragons in the waters. It was Yahweh who crushed and broke the heads of leviathan and gave him to be meat, food, to the creatures inhabiting the desert wilderness. It was Yahweh who opened up springs and streams, creating fountain and flood; He dried up the mighty and ever-flowing rivers. The day and the night are Yahweh's, for it is He who established the sun and moon. He set all the boundaries of the earth, and made both summer and winter.

> The oldest creation myth in the Bible isn't in Genesis. It is alluded to in Isaiah, Job and the Psalms. The clearest and fullest biblical account of this ancient myth appears in Ps 74.

In the east, in a mountain sanctuary near the steppe known as Eden, Yahweh had planted a garden to be a paradise of pleasure. He made all kinds of trees grow out of the ground—trees that were pleasing to the eye and good for food. In the middle of the garden were planted the Tree of Life and the Tree of the Knowledge of Good and Evil. A river flowed out of Eden to water the garden, and from there the river sank into the ground; later re-emerging to become the four heads of the rivers: Pishon, which winds its way through the entire land of Havilah; the Gihon, which winds through the entire land of Cush; and the last two, the Chidekel, or Tigris, which runs along the east side of Ashur, and the Phirath, known by some as the Euphrates.

Yahweh looked at His creation and said; "Let us make human beings, in our likeness, in our image, so that they may rule over the fish in the sea and the birds in the sky, and over all the creatures on the ground." And so Yahweh made human beings, as He said, in His image: creating both male and female. Yahweh formed them from the dust of the ground and breathed into their nostrils His name, the Divine Name, giving them the breath of life. For this reason, it is wrong to say that because human beings are so unworthy, and the name of God is so holy, that they should not dare to speak it: for each moment of every breath humans take, for every moment they are alive, they do so with the name of God on their lips. The male Yahweh made was named Adam, for he was formed from the ground, and the other, the female, had long enchanting golden hair, and was called Lilith.

Yahweh put the first humans into the garden and taught them that the plant world, of which trees are the most significant, transforms the earth from a barren and lifeless mass, into an environment capable of supporting other forms of life. He taught them that a wise and understanding person does not destroy something so worthy but protects it from destruction and damage, while taking benefit from it. He took and led them around all the trees of the Garden; showing them how to take care of it and said, "Look at My works, how beautiful and praiseworthy they are! And all this that I have created, I created for you. Pay attention that you do not corrupt and destroy My world: if you corrupt it, there is no one to repair it after you. You are free to eat from any tree in the garden; but you must not eat from the Tree of the Knowledge of Good and Evil, for when you eat from it you will certainly die."

> Though Lilith is not in our Genesis account, there is still memory of her within Scripture, with Isaiah (34:14) referencing her.

Sadly, Adam and Lilith never found peace together. One day Lilith saw some of the fruit that had fallen from the tree of the Knowledge of Good and Evil and lay rotting on the ground, and she quietly ate some of it. Soon the human couple began to quarrel, and this quarrelling grew in frequency. Their quarrelling wrestled over the issue of patriarchal authority: an idea that Adam was beginning to develop, and a matriarchal desire Lilith had for emancipation. Lilith perceived herself as an equal to Adam and her consciousness of equality was a natural thought process. Anything less than equality was unthought-of, unthinkable, and unnatural.

It came to pass that during one of these conflicts Adam desired sexual intimacy with Lilith, but she was not inclined to engage in the manner he so desired, taking offence at the recumbent position he demanded. Lilith turned away shaking her head arguing; "I will not lie below you, why must I?" Adam countered her bluntly stating; "I will not lie beneath you, but only above you, only on top! For you are fit only to be below me in the bottom position, and I, well, I am to be the superior one above you." This made Lilith both frustrated and angry. She responded with a stamp of her foot; "We are both equal because we both come from the earth, for I was also made from dust just as you were!" It was an argument that neither would attempt to solve or compromise on.

So neither listened to the other for Adam could not cope with her desire for freedom, and Lilith would settle for nothing less, and when Adam tried to compel her obedience by force, Lilith recognized the tyranny for what it was, and immediately resisted. Lilith, now in a rage, used knowledge she had gained from eating the fruit of the Tree of the Knowledge of Good and Evil, and uttered the magic name of God, sprouted wings and took off into the air and left him.

Lilith went and settled by the Red Sea, the place that would one day become the transition point of the Jews from the security of bondage in Egypt to the insecurity of freedom in the desert, and in whose powerful waters the Egyptians were destined to perish. The Red Sea was a region abounding in lascivious demons. There, Lilith met the archangel Samael, (who is also called the 'Great Demon'). Samael was not a good angel, and though he is a fallen angel, still remains Yahweh's servant to this day. Lilith and Samael settled down together before Samael returned to his home in the seventh heaven.

While Lilith and Samael were settling down together Adam complained to Yahweh saying; "I have been deserted by my helpmeet; she has fled the Garden." Yahweh, believing Adam, sent the angels Senoy, Sansenoy and Semangelof to fetch Lilith back. When they found her beside the Red Sea, Lilith was giving birth to night spirits, known as 'lilim' at the rate of more than one hundred a day. The angels went to her and said; "Return to Adam without delay or we will drown you!" Even though Lilith was the one who left, she felt rejected and angry. For independence and freedom from tyranny, Lilith was willing to forsake the economic security of returning to the Garden, even if it meant accepting loneliness and exclusion. Lilith gestured around and at herself, and asked; "How can I return to Adam and live like an honest housewife, after my stay beside the Red Sea?" The angels, seeing the change in circumstance and situation, quickly reported back to Yahweh. Yahweh went and said to Adam; "If she wants to return, all the better. If not, she will have to accept that one hundred of her children will die every day, for the natural lifespan of a lilim is very short." Then Yahweh sent the angels back to Lilith.

> The angels' Senoy, Sansenoy and Semangelof are seen as safeguards against Lilith's actions towards mother's and newborns. The onomatopoeic sound of their names said together: resembling sounds like the hiss of a snake or the crackle of fire, warns Lilith that she should not approach.

Senoy, Sansenoy and Semangelof returned to her and spoke in such a way that angels do: giving a statement assuming the human understands the context and the reasoning behind their message, whilst at the same time not truly grasping the words that Yahweh had spoken. They said to her; "It will be death to refuse!" Still, Lilith refused to return to the Garden, and especially to Adam. Seeing so many of her own children dying and feeling it was a punishment, responded to the angels claiming that she felt she was created to devour human children. Senoy, Sansenoy and Semangelof decided to try and drown Lilith, and to prevent the three angels from drowning her in the Red Sea, Lilith swore in the name of God to not harm any child who wore an amulet bearing her name. Lilith still dwells in chaotic, desert lands where the soil is infertile and wild animals roam, attempting to kill newborn children out of the twisted spite that has grown up within her. She does so in retaliation for Adam's mistreatment of her and because she feels that Yahweh is responsible for the deaths of the lilim. Yet Yahweh still holds out hope of her return, for by allowing her to forge an agreement with the angels, He demonstrated that she is not totally separated from the Divine.

While Yahweh had been waiting for Senoy, Sansenoy and Semangelof to return with Lilith's answer, Yahweh brought all the animals and birds to Adam to see what he would name them; and whatever he called each living creature, that was its name. When they passed before him in pairs, male and female, Adam, being already like a twenty-year-old man, felt jealous of their loves, and though he tried coupling with each female creature in turn, found no satisfaction in the act. He therefore cried; "Every creature but I has a proper mate!" and prayed Yahweh would remedy this injustice. When Yahweh heard and saw all that was happening, and had received the news of Lilith's decision, He said; "It is not good for the man to be alone. I will make a helper suitable for him." Yahweh put Adam into a deep sleep; and while he was sleeping, Yahweh took one of the man's ribs, a part close to the heart: the seat of the emotions and soul, and then closed up the *place with flesh. Yahweh then made a woman from the rib. He did so as a sign of intimacy and equality for being of his side: neither above nor below, she was to be an equal. Here was an attempt to create harmony.*

When Yahweh brought her to Adam he exclaimed; "This is now bone of my bones and flesh of my flesh; she shall be called Eve, for she was taken out of man." They both then continued in the Garden. Though they were naked, they knew no shame for they were clothed in light. Yet it was not long before Adam began pushing his stance of patriarchal authority. Adam's patriarchal effort ultimately proved disastrous, for as Adam showed Eve around the Garden, he told her of the rule not to eat from the Tree of the Knowledge of Good and Evil, but Adam extended the original prohibition to include not touching it, and in doing so left Eve believing that the extension was also of Divine origin and not an exaggeration he had made up.

Now in the Garden there was a serpent. Serpent was craftier than any other wild animal that Yahweh had made, and Samael had seduced Serpent to evil. One day as Adam and Eve were standing together near the middle of the Garden, Serpent said to Eve; "Did Yahweh say; 'You shall not eat from any tree in the garden?" Eve in her innocence replied; "We may eat of the fruit of the trees in the garden; but Yahweh has said, we are not to eat of the fruit of the tree that is in the middle of the garden, nor touch it, for if we do, we shall die!"

But Serpent retorted; "You will not die; for Yahweh knows that when you eat of it your eyes will be opened, and you will be gods and know good and evil."

To prove this, Serpent showed Eve that the extension to not touch the tree could be flouted with impunity by using its skinny little legs to climb the tree and coil itself into the branches. Adam followed on silently and did not admit to his folly. This led Eve to believe that the entire prohibition would not be enforced, and so when she saw that the tree was good for food, and that it was a delight to the eyes, and that the tree was to be desired to make one  wise, she took of its fruit and began eating it as she passed some over to Adam who also ate it. Suddenly, their eyes were opened, the light that covered them faded, and they knew that they were naked. They then sewed fig leaves together, and made loincloths for themselves.

Later that day as the evening breeze began blowing gently, Adam and Eve heard Yahweh walking in the Garden and they hid themselves amongst trees hoping Yahweh would go on by and ignore them. Serpent looked on from a nearby tree with interest as instead of simply walking on by, Yahweh instead called out; "Adam, where are you?" Adam stepped forward slightly and replied; "I heard the sound of you in the garden, and I was afraid, because I was naked; and so I hid myself." Yahweh paused for a moment, tilted His head slightly to one side and said slowly; "Who told you that you were naked? Have you eaten from the tree of which I commanded you not to eat?" Adam realised that he could be in a lot of trouble for what he had done, and so attempted to shift the blame to Eve. Pulling her out from the trees and pushing her forward, Adam said hurriedly; "Eve, this woman whom you gave to me, she, she gave me fruit from the tree, and only then did I eat it." Then Yahweh looked at Eve and said to her; "What is this that you have done?" Not understanding the extent of the deceit of Adam, Eve pointed over to Serpent and said; "Serpent tricked me, and I ate." Yahweh was not impressed, and though He had tried to create a place of harmony and gentleness, He realised this was not to be.

Yahweh said to Serpent;

"Because you have done this, you are cursed among all animals and the wild creatures; upon your belly you shall go, and all the days of your life you shall eat dust. I will put animosity and enmity between you and the woman, and between both your descendants. Her descendants will strike your head, and you will strike their heel."

Yahweh said to Eve;

"I will sharpen the pain of your pregnancy, and in pain you will give birth. You will desire to control your husband, but instead he will rule over you."

Yahweh said to Adam;

"Since you listened to your wife and ate from the tree whose fruit I commanded you not to eat, the ground is cursed because of you, and through sweaty hard work you shall eat of it all the days of your life, and It will grow thorns and thistles for you. By the sweat of your face you shall eat bread until you return to the ground, for out of it you were taken; you are dust, and so to dust you shall return."

After uttering these harsh punishments to Adam, Eve, and Serpent, for their failure to heed the one explicit prohibition that governed human life in the Garden, Yahweh felt a fleeting expression of sorrow over the fate that awaited humanity outside the Garden and displayed an act of tenderness. For though Adam and Eve were clothed in loincloths made from fig leaves, Yahweh made them garments. Serpent's legs had been removed so that Serpent now crawled on the ground. Serpent could no longer talk, and had the serpent not been punished, Serpent would have been a servant to humanity. But as these changes were coming over Serpent, in a great change and shedding, Yahweh made garments from the skin of the serpent that had just been punished for giving Eve the fruit.

The walking, talking Serpent had now been transformed into the slithering silent creature that snakes are. Then Yahweh sighed saying; "See, the human beings have become like one of us, knowing good and evil; and now, they might reach out their hands and also take from the Tree of Life, and eat, and live forever". Therefore Yahweh sent Adam and Eve out from the Garden of Eden, to till the ground from which Adam was taken. Yahweh had the angel Jophiel, one of the cherubim, drive Adam and Eve out to the east of the Garden, and then had Jophiel with a flaming sword in hand, guard the way to the Tree of Life. Yahweh chose Jophiel, whose name means 'Beauty of God', in order that having been sent forth from the Garden that human beings would forever carry with them the remembrance that justice was tempered with mercy, and have imprinted upon their last memory of this garden paradise a vision, not of the terrible frown of an angry God, but of the beauty of goodness which was grieved and, like the offer to Lilith, that they are not totally separated from the Divine, and one day could be reconciled.

Sadly the trees no longer exist in the Garden, for the Garden is no more. Over time, the Garden degenerated and trees, plants and animals withered and died. The cherubim who had to guard the Tree of Life while in the Garden then lifted up the tree and took it to safety in God's heavenly realm in order to preserve it without the contamination of age, sin, and death which now inhabit the world.

This garden existed a long time ago in a land far, far away. But all is not lost. Scriptures tell us that spirits, who can exert influences over us, as they have done so to our ancestors, inhabit trees. These trees were known as elon moreh: instructing trees. The "instructing tree" outside of Nablus seems to have been the most important of these instructing trees, and is mentioned numerous times in the Bible. Abraham visited it, Jacob buried idols under it, Abimelech was crowned there, and Joshua assembled the People of Israel by it and placed the written covenant between them and Yahweh etched in stone beneath it.

All over the world, and even here, there are places where gardens of trees still grow that draw us back to the Garden of Eden and remind us, in their offering of a place of peace, calm, and inner safety. The spirits of these trees draw from the roots of the great tree of life and if we are very quiet, and very still, we may feel them speaking to us.

QUESTIONS TO PONDER

- When reflecting on what you know of the story of Adam and Eve, I wonder what questions the differences in these stories raises for you.

- I wonder how do you react towards Adam's behaviour regarding Eve, especially in light of how he treated Lilith.

- Reviewing Adam's behaviour, what tools of manipulation and control can you see?

- Where in this story do you see trauma, and what are its effects?

- I wonder what in this story unsettles you the most.

- I wonder how we can minister to people who have experienced the types of trauma identifiable in this story.

MURDER

Adam knew his wife, Eve, and from this sexual union, Eve conceived. Adam was not in the company of Eve during the time of her pregnancy as he was off in the east and she in the west. When the days of Eve to be delivered were fulfilled, and she began to feel the pangs of labour, she prayed to Yahweh for help. But He appeared not to answer her supplications.

"Who will carry the report to my lord Adam?" she asked herself. "You luminaries in the sky, I beg you, tell it to my master Adam when you return to the east!"

In that self-same hour, Adam cried out; "The lamentation of Eve has pierced to my ear! Mayhap Serpent has again assaulted her." and he hastened to his wife. Finding her in grievous pain, he pleaded with Yahweh on her behalf, and twelve angels, together with two heavenly *powers, appeared. All these took up their post to her right and left, while Michael (the archangel), standing on her right side, passed his hand over her; from her face downward to her breast, and said; "Be blessed, Eve, for the sake of Adam. Because of his solicitations and his prayers I was sent to grant you our assistance. Make ready to give birth to your child!"*

Immediately their first baby boy was born. He was a radiant figure. Eve, speaking with joy of the birth of her son, named him Cain exclaiming; 'I have acquired a man with the help of God'. The name Cain, when it is interpreted, signifies a Possession. Adam took Eve and the boy to his home in the east. God sent him various kinds of seeds by the hand of the archangel Michael, and Cain was taught how to cultivate the ground and make it yield produce and fruits, to sustain himself, his family, and his posterity.

Then Adam and Eve had another son, Cain's little brother, and they named him Abel. The name Abel signifies Sorrow. In a dream, Eve had seen the blood of Abel flow into the mouth of Cain, who drank it with avidity, though his brother entreated him not to take all. When she told her dream to Adam, he said lamentingly; "O that this may not portend the death of Abel at the hand of Cain!" He separated the two boys, assigning to each an abode of his own, and taught each a different occupation. When Cain got older he became a farmer, a tiller of the ground. When Abel grew up he became a shepherd, keeping sheep.

One day, at the insistence of Adam, Cain and Abel brought gifts to Yahweh to thank Him for all the good things He had done for them. Cain brought some of the things he had grown. Abel brought the first lamb born to one of his sheep. It was the best in his flock. Yahweh was happy with Abel's gift, because He saw that Abel really wanted to please Him and always do what Yahweh wanted, and so He accepted it by sending heavenly fire down to consume it. But Yahweh knew that Cain wasn't so sure he wanted to do what God wanted. Before the sacrifice, Cain ate his meal first, and after he had satisfied his own appetite, offered to Yahweh what was left over: a few bad grains of corn seed. So Yahweh wasn't happy with Cain's gift and that made Cain mad.

According to some Rabbis, all good souls are derived from Abel, and all bad souls from Cain. Cain's soul was derived from Satan, his body alone was from Eve; for the evil spirit Samael according to some, Satan according to others, deceived Eve and thus Cain was the son of the evil one. See 1 John 3:12

Yahweh loved Cain, and He said to him; "Why are you scowling? If you always do what is right, you will be happy, and I will accept you. But be careful. Bad thoughts will ruin your life; wrongdoing is not far from your thoughts. Learn to control them."

But Cain didn't listen to God. Instead he blamed his brother. And even though Yahweh loved both brothers as much as anyone could ever be loved, Cain thought Yahweh loved Abel more than him. So from that day on, Cain began to think mean things about his younger brother. He kept thinking them and thinking them. And the more he thought them, the harder it was to stop. And the more he thought them, the meaner his thoughts became. Until one day he planned a terrible thing! He said to his brother; "Abel, come with me out into the fields." Abel went because he loved and trusted his brother. And so they walked out into the fields. And when Cain got Abel out where nobody could see or hear them, he took a rock and he killed Abel.

Later Yahweh found Cain out working and asked; "Where is Abel?" "How should I know?" Cain replied. "Am I supposed to take care of my brother?" But Yahweh knew the terrible thing Cain had done. Yahweh said to him; "I see your brother's blood on the ground and it cries out to me! Because you have spilled your brother's blood into the ground, the ground won't grow your crops for you anymore. From now on you will have to wander in far away places to find your food." "Lord, the punishment is too hard for me!" Cain said. "This day you have driven me away from the soil, and I shall be hidden from your face; I shall be a fugitive and a wanderer on the earth. You bear the whole world, is my sin so great that you cannot bear it also? This iniquity is too great for me, yet yesterday you banished my father from your presence, and now today you banish me. In truth it will be said; 'Yahweh's way is to banish'."

Although this was not true repentance, for Cain did not regret what he had done, only that he had been caught out, Yahweh granted Cain some leniency, and removed half of his chastisement from him: originally, Yahweh's decree had condemned Cain to be a fugitive and a wanderer on the earth, now Cain was no longer to roam about forever, though he would remain a fugitive. Cain pressed on; "My relatives will try to kill me when they hear what I have done. I will always be running." And Yahweh responded saying to him; "Therefore whoever kills Cain, vengeance shall be taken on them sevenfold". So Yahweh put a mark on Cain to protect him, so that none finding him should kill him. Yahweh also gave him a dog as a protection against the wild beasts.

On that sad, sad day, Cain left his only home and family. Because of the evil thing Cain had done, Adam and Eve lost not just one son, but two. Cain went out and away from Yahweh and dwelt in the land, a place of wandering to the east of Eden. Cain's crime had baneful consequences, not for himself alone, but like the flow-on effects *of all actions of envy and jealousy, the whole of nature was affected also.*

Before Cain had committed this sad and horrible crime, the fruits that the earth had produced when he tilled the ground had tasted like the fruits of the Garden. Now his labour produced nothing but thorns and thistles. The ground changed and deteriorated at the very moment of Abel's violent end at Cain's hand. The trees and the plants in the part of the earth where Abel had lived also refused to yield their fruits on account of their grief over him. This lasted until the birth of Seth. But never did they resume their former powers. While, before, the vine had borne nine hundred and twenty-six different varieties of fruit, it now brought forth but one kind. And so it was with all other species. They will regain their pristine powers only in the world to come.

The burial of Abel's corpse also modified nature. For a long time it lay upon the ground exposed, simply because Adam and Eve did not know what to do with it. While the faithful dog of Abel kept guard that birds and beasts did no harm to his body, Adam and Eve sat beside it and wept. On a sudden, Adam and Eve were distracted by a sound nearby. Looking up, they observed how a raven scratched the earth away in one spot, and then hid in the ground the body of a dead, fellow raven. So Adam, following the example of the raven, buried the body of Abel, and God rewarded the raven.

The young of a raven are born with white feathers, wherefore the old birds desert them, not recognizing them as their offspring. They take them for serpents. God feeds them until their plumage turns black, and the parent birds return to them. As an additional reward, when the ravens pray for rain Yahweh grants their petition.

After Cain had travelled over many countries, he built a city, named Nod, and there he settled his abode. While out there Cain knew his wife, and she conceived, and bore Enoch. However, although Cain had accepted his punishment from Yahweh, he did not accept it in order to amend or atone for his actions, but rather to increase his wickedness: for he only aimed to procure every thing that was for his own bodily pleasure, though it obliged him to be injurious to his neighbours. He augmented his household substance with much wealth, by rapine and violence: he excited his acquaintances to procure pleasure and spoils by robbery: and became a great leader of men into wicked courses. He also introduced a change in that way of simplicity wherein men lived before. Cain was the creator of measures and weights. And whereas people lived innocently and generously while they knew nothing of such arts, Cain changed the world into cunning craftiness. He first of all set boundaries about lands: he built a city, and fortified it with walls: and he compelled his family to come together to it: and called that city Enoch, after the name of his son.

Jude 1:11; "Woe to them! For they have traveled down Cain's path", is based on the Jewish tradition that Cain was a corrupting influence, enticing others into his pattern of misdeeds. Cain's corrupting jealousy is seen in false teachers: a jealousy of those who obeyed the Lord, which grows into hated of genuine believers.

QUESTIONS TO PONDER

- When reflecting on what you know of the story of Cain and Abel, I wonder what questions the differences in these stories raises for you.

- I wonder how do you react towards Cain's behaviour.

- Reviewing Cain's behaviour, what tools of manipulation and abuse can you see?

- If we are not careful, being angry and jealous can lead us to hurt people, even if we do not mean to. I wonder about examples of this sort of behaviour ruling our lives and the consequences we have had to live with.

- Where in this story do you see trauma, and what are its effects?

- I wonder what in this story unsettles you the most.

- I wonder how we can minister to people who have experienced the types of trauma identifiable in this story.

THE WIFE AND THE HANDMAID

Our world is full of examples of innocents suffering for the sins of others. At times the actions of great religious leaders, like Abraham, have ruined their ability and testimonies before pagan royal courts, and have caused people to suffer.

Terah, along with Lot, his grandson, (whose father Haran had died), and Abram, his son, and Sarai (Abram's wife, who on account of not having child was thought barren) set out from Ur of the Chaldees, heading towards the land of Canaan. They came to Charan, and dwelt there.

One day, Yahweh said to Abram; "I want you to go forth from this land and from your kindred and the house of your father, and go into the land which I show you. I will make you become a great nation, and I will bless you, and make your name great; and you shall be a blessing. And I bless those blessing you, and I curse those who are disesteeming of you. In you, all the families of the earth shall be blessed."

So as Yahweh had spoken, Abram did. Abram left, taking Sarai his wife, and Lot his brother's son, (whom Abram was guiding to be his heir), and all their possessions that they had gained; the persons that they had obtained in Charan, and they set out for the land of Canaan. When they had come to the land of Canaan, Abram passed through the land to the place at Shechem, to the oak of Moreh; and the Canaanite was then in the land.

Whilst there, Yahweh appeared to Abram and said; "I will give this land to your offspring." And so Abram built an alter on the spot where Yahweh had appeared. Abram removed himself from there and went towards a mountain at the east of Beth-El, and stretched out the tent (Beth-El at the west, and Hai at the east), and also built there an alter to Yahweh, and began preaching about Him. Then Abram journeyed by stages toward the Negeb.

But it was not long after Yahweh's great promise to Abram that a grievous famine broke out in the land. So Abram packed up his tent and took his family south, down to Egypt. Though Abram had displayed great faith and considerable courage in trusting Yahweh when he left his home city, on the borders of Egypt Abram began to grow afraid, and started to weave plans for his own safety, even at the risk of others. So as they drew near to enter Egypt, Abram said to Sarai; "Listen, I tell you! I know that you are a beautiful and attractive woman, so when the Egyptians see you, they will say, 'This is his wife'; and they will slay me, killing me stone dead, to acquire you, but you, they will let you live. So you are to say to them that you are my sister, so that things will go well for me for your sake, and my life will be spared because of you." Lot followed along with Abram's plan, encouraged Sarai to go along with it and remained silent, not revealing their secret. And so it came to pass that after Abram entered into Egypt, that the Egyptians did see Sarai; and that she was exceeding fair and beautiful. Abram was now in a land Yahweh had not commanded him to go to, and without trust, honour and from a fear of the consequences, Abram, along with Lot, misled the Egyptians and was willing to subject Sarai to sexual liaisons in order that he would survive economically. This included princes of Pharaoh, who after seeing her, and speaking with Lot, went back and praised her to Pharaoh. So Pharaoh ordered his servants to bring Sarai before his presence. And Pharaoh saw for himself the beauty of Sarai, and he was greatly pleased. He rejoiced greatly at Sarai's presence and gave gifts to all those that brought him the news concerning her, and so the woman was taken, with Abram's consent, for the purpose of marriage into Pharaoh's harem. Because of this, Pharaoh treated Abram well for her sake; and Abram acquired sheep, oxen, male and female donkeys, male servants and female handmaids, and camels.

Because of Pharaoh's infatuation with Sarai, he wrote in her marriage document giving her wealth, in silver and gold, and he wrote giving her the land of Goshen for a possession. Therefore the children of Israel dwelt in the land of Goshen, in the land of their mother Sarai. Pharaoh also gave her Hagar, his daughter from a concubine, as her handmaid. Yahweh plagued Pharaoh and his house with severe sores and wounds, over the matter of Sarai: Abram's wife. Sarai though, was not afflicted.

This is the Bible's first mention of Egypt as a nation: the ancient name of Egypt is Mizraim, one of Noah's grandsons.

When Pharaoh found out the reason for their affliction, (because he had taken another man's wife), Pharaoh summoned Abram, and berated Abram for his actions, saying; "What is this you have done to me? Why have you not declared to me that she is your wife? Why have you said, 'She is my sister', and I take her to myself for a wife? So now, then behold, here is your wife, take her and go!"

Pharaoh commanded his men concerning Abram; and they escorted him on his way, with his wife and all that he had: his sheep and cattle, male and female donkeys, male and female servants, camels, and silver and gold.

So Abram went up out of Egypt, (he and his wife and all that he had, and Lot with him), into the Negev (the South country of Judah). Because of the gifts of Pharaoh Abram was now extremely rich in livestock and in silver and in gold. Abram journeyed on from the Negev as far as Bethel, to the place where his tent had been at the beginning, between Beth-El and Hai, where he had first built an altar;

> Unfortunately, Abraham didn't learn from this episode and repeats the same behaviour in Genesis 20 with Abimelech, King of Gerar.

and there, Abram called on Yahweh in prayer, and began preaching. Lot, who went with Abram, now also had flocks and herds and tents.

Now though, the land was not able to sustain all their grazing and water needs while they lived near one another, for their possessions were too great for them to stay together.

There was strife and quarrelling between the herdsmen of Abram's cattle and the herdsmen of Lot's cattle. Now the Canaanite and the

Perizzite were living in the land at that same time and that made grazing the livestock difficult too. Abram's shepherds abided strictly by the rules given to them by their pious master concerning trespassing upon the property of others, but Lot's shepherds were rough men who did not. Thus there were constant arguments and strife between the herdsmen of Abram and Lot. Soon complaints reached Abram. Abram, realizing that the quarrel between the shepherds would eventually lead to an estrangement between him and Lot, though he were the senior, offered Lot the choice of the areas available. So Abram said to Lot; "Please let there be no strife between us, or between your herdsmen and mine, because we are family. Is not the entire land before you? Please let us part and separate yourself from me. If you take the left, then I will go to the right; or if you choose the right, then I will go to the left."

Abram could have driven Lot away by force but chose not to: showing that material possessions were not uppermost in his system of values. Lot though, was unabashed in choosing the most fertile land. So Lot lifted up his eyes, looked about and saw that the valley of the Jordan was a well watered land — (this was before Yahweh destroyed Sodom and Gomorrah); in some ways it was very much like the Garden, or like the land of Egypt, as you go to Zoar at the south end of the Dead Sea. Then Lot chose for himself the whole the valley of the Jordan; and Abram and Lot were separated from each other.

Abram settled in the land of Canaan, and Lot settled in the cities of the valley

---

In the Ancient Near East the custom was that the more powerful of the two would allow the lesser to make the choice, knowing that the lesser, who understood the rules, would take the lesser part.

Against convention, Lot chose what he thought was the best portion.

of the Jordan and camped as far as Sodom and lived there. But the men of Sodom were extremely wicked and unashamedly sinful against Yahweh.

After Lot had left him, Yahweh said to Abram; "Now lift up your eyes and look from the place where you are, northward and southward and eastward and westward; for the whole of the land which you are seeing, I will give to you and to your descendants forever. I will make your descendants as the dust of the earth, so that, if a man is able to number the dust of the earth, even so will your descendants be numbered. Arise, go up and down through the land, to its length, and to its breadth, for to you I give it." Then Abram broke camp and moved his tent, and came and settled amongst the great grove of the terebinth trees of Mamre, which are in Hebron, and there he built an altar to Yahweh. But Abram was sad.

Yahweh came to Abram in a vision; "Do not be afraid, Abram. I am your sovereign; your reward will be very great."

But Abram said; "Sovereign Yahweh, what can you give me since I remain childless and the one who will inherit my estate is Eliezer of Damascus? You have given me no children; so a servant in my household will be my heir."

Yahweh replied saying; "This man Eliezer will not be your heir, but a son coming from your own body will be your heir." Yahweh took Abram outside and said; "Look up at the heavens and count the stars: if indeed you can count them." Then Yahweh said; "So shall your descendants be." Abram believed Yahweh, and He credited it to him as righteousness.

Sarai was aware of how Abram was feeling, and resenting the fact he had no heir of his own, particularly as she, his wife, had not borne any children. Sarai still had Hagar, the Egyptian handmaid, so she said to Abram; "Yahweh appears to have kept me from having children, so why don't you just have intercourse with my handmaid; perhaps I can build up a family from her." Abram listened to Sarai.

And so it was that at the end of the tenth year of Abram's dwelling in the land of Canaan, Sarai, Abram's wife, took Hagar the Egyptian, her handmaid, and gave her to Abram her husband, for a wife.

After Abram had intercourse with Hagar, she conceived. When Hagar knew she was pregnant, she began to despise her mistress.

Sarai said to Abram; "You are responsible for the wrong I am suffering. I put my servant in your arms, and now that she knows she is pregnant, she despises me. May Yahweh judge between you and me." Abram said back to Sarai; "Your handmaid is in your hand, do to her that which is good in your eyes." and so Sarai afflicted and mistreated her, and Hagar fled from her presence.

A messenger of Yahweh found Hagar by the fountain of water in the wilderness, by the fountain beside the road to Shur. He said; "Hagar, Sarai's handmaid, whence have you come, and whither do you go?' Hagar said; "I am fleeing from the presence of Sarai, my mistress."

The messenger of Yahweh said to her; "Go back to your mistress, and humble yourself under her hands. I will so increase your descendants that they will be too numerous to count. You have conceived and are bearing a son. Call his name Ishmael, (which means 'God hears'), for Yahweh heard your affliction." The messenger considered the future and continued; "He will be a wild-ass man: his hand against every one, and every one's hand against him, and he will live to the east in hostility toward all his brothers."

And Hagar gave this name to the messenger of Yahweh who spoke to her; "You are the God who sees me," for she said; "I have now seen the back of the One who sees me." That is why the well was called Beer Lahai Roi (which means 'well of the Living One who sees me'). It is still there, between Kadesh and Bered.

So Hagar returned and bore Abram a son and called him Ishmael. Some time later Yahweh said to Abram; "Sarai your wife, I will bless and will surely give you a son by her. I will bless her so that she will be the mother of nations; kings of peoples will come from her."

Abram fell facedown; laughed and said to himself; "Will a son be born to a man who is old? Will Sarah bear a child?" Abram said to Yahweh; "If only Ishmael might live under your blessing!"

But Yahweh said; "But your wife Sarai will bear you a son, and you will call him Isaac (which means 'he laughs'). I will establish my *covenant with him as an everlasting covenant for his descendants after him. As for Ishmael, I have heard you: I will surely bless him; I will make him fruitful and will greatly increase his numbers. He will be the father of twelve rulers, and I will make him into a great nation. But my covenant I will establish with Isaac, whom Sarah will bear to you by this time next year."*

Yahweh was gracious to Sarai as he had said, and did as promised. Sarai became pregnant and bore a son to Abram in his old age, at the very time Yahweh had said. Sarai said; "Yahweh has brought me laughter, and everyone who hears about this will laugh with me." And she added; "Who would have said to Abram that Sarai would nurse children? Yet I have borne him a son in his old age." Abram named the boy Isaac, and when his son Isaac was eight days old, Abram circumcised him.

Isacc grew and was weaned, and on the day Isaac was weaned Abram held a great feast. But Sarai saw that the son whom Hagar the Egyptian had borne to Abraham was mocking, and she said to Abram; "Get rid of that slave woman and her son, for that slave woman's son will never share in the inheritance with my son Isaac."

The matter distressed Abraham greatly because it concerned his son, but Yahweh said to him; "Do not be so distressed about the boy and your maidservant. Listen to whatever Sarai tells you, because it is through Isaac that your descendants will be reckoned. I will make the son of the maidservant into a nation also, because he is your offspring."

So early the next morning Abram took some food and a skin of water and gave them to Hagar. He set them on her shoulders and then sent her off with the boy. She went on her way and wandered in the desert of Beersheba. When the water in the skin was gone, she put the boy under one of the bushes. Then she went off and sat down nearby, about a bowshot away, for she thought, "I cannot watch the boy die." And as she sat there the child began to sob. Yahweh heard the boy crying, and an angel of Yahweh called to Hagar from heaven and said to her; "What is the matter, Hagar? Do not be afraid; Yahweh has heard the boy crying as he lies there. Lift the boy up and take him by the hand, for I will make him into a great nation."

Then God opened her eyes and she saw a well of water. So she went and filled the skin with water and gave the boy a drink. God was with the boy as he grew up. He lived in the desert and became an archer.

QUESTIONS TO PONDER

- When reflecting on what you know of the story of Abram (Abraham) and Sarai (Sarah), I wonder what questions the differences in these stories raises for you.

- I wonder how do you react towards Abram's behaviour.

- Reviewing how the different characters behave, what tools of manipulation and abuse can you see?

- Where in this story do you see trauma, and what are its effects?

- I wonder what in this story unsettles you the most.

- I wonder how we can minister to people who have experienced the types of trauma identifiable in this story.

SODOM

Troubling and terrible stories of Sodom began to reach Yahweh. Sodom had no consideration for the poor or for the passing stranger. To a passing stranger they would offer no hospitality; nor even sell him any food or water.

The judges of Sodom and Gomorrah had beds erected in the public streets of the cities. When a traveller came to tarry in their cities, they would seize upon him and put him into one of those bedsteads by force. And if he was shorter than the bedstead, six men would lay hands on him and stretch him until he was equal in length; and if he was taller then they would press him against the two sides of the bedstead until he would fit. And they did not give ear to the cries of the strangers but tortured them until they almost reached the gates of death, when they would say; "So it will be done to everyone that enters into our land". And all the people hearing of what was done in the cities of Sodom, kept away from coming into these places.

When a poor man came into any of their cities they were extremely liberal with their charity. They opened their hands and gave the needy and destitute silver and gold in great abundance. And after that, they caused it to be proclaimed in a loud voice throughout all their territory that no one dare to give that poor man a morsel of bread for all the money he might offer. And since no man could get out of the land before many days, the poor man had to die of starvation, for no one would give him a morsel of bread in all their cities. And when the poor man was dead, all those that gave him their silver and gold came and recognized it and got it back. And they took away the garments off the poor man and fought over them, and whosoever was strongest took all the garments for themself. And after the corpse was stripped of its garments, they buried it in its nudity into one of the ditches of the deserts around them.

Once they had found out that Paltith, (one of Lot's daughters), had secretly given food to a stranger who was near starvation. Paltith, having compassion for the poor stranger, supplied him secretly with bread for many days, and so he was kept alive. When Paltith went out to fetch water, she would hide the bread in her water-pitcher and when she came to the place of the poor man she took the bread and placed it before him. When three Sodomites saw her doing this, they seized Paltith and the bread and dragged her before their judges. Finding her guilty they kindled a fire in the streets, cast her into it, and burnt her to ashes. Another time, when they discovered that a young girl had fed a starving beggar, they stripped her of all her vestments and anointed her with honey from the crown of her head to the sole of her foot. They placed her upon the city wall, so that she died from the stings of the bees attracted by the honey. Her body swelled up *and the poor girl cried out in her pain (caused by the bee stings) but no one would regard her cries and no one would have mercy upon her. Her shrieks of agony went up to heaven. Hearing these, and worse, Yahweh said; "Because the outcry against Sodom and Gomorrah is great and their sin is very grave, I will go down to see whether they have done altogether according to the outcry which has come to Me; and if not, I will know."*

Yahweh sent three angels. They rested with Abram and shared a meal in his tent. One, named Michael, spoke with Abram and told him what Yahweh planned to do. Abram begged that they spare the city if there be even ten innocents living there. The angel Michael agreed to spare the city to save the innocent. But there would not be even ten innocents within the city. Michael returned to Yahweh. The other two angels, Gabriel and Raphael, continued on to Sodom: Gabriel to overthrow Sodom, and Raphael to rescue Lot (on account of Abram).

The two angels arrived at Sodom in the evening; and Lot was sitting in the gate of Sodom, for he had become a civic leader in the city. Lot had from the outset, decided to dwell in Sodom because he wanted to engage in the licentious behaviour of its inhabitants, but he had not completely forgotten his uncle Abram's teachings and ways of living and had not quite accepted the Sodomite attitude towards strangers and their cruel treatment of the unfortunate passer-by.

> Yahweh will later judge Judah saying; 'look at the guilt of your sister Sodom: she and her daughters were proud, sated with food, complacent in prosperity. They did not give any help to the poor and needy. They were arrogant and did detestable things before me; then, as you have seen, I removed them.'
> Ezekiel 16:49-50

When Lot saw the two approach, he rose to meet them, and bowed himself with his face to the ground, and said, "My lords, turn aside, I pray you, to your servant's house and spend the night, and wash your feet; then you may rise up early and go on your way." They said; "No; we will spend the night in the street." But Lot urged them strongly; so they turned aside to him and entered his house. Lot's wife though, did not want them in the house, and only grudgingly admitted them. As an act of hospitality, as Abram had done, Lot asked his wife to bring the guests salt. She responded; "Do you even wish to learn this bad habit from Abram?" She finally complied with her husband's request, but acted cunningly in order to remove the guests from her house. She went to her women neighbours to borrow the salt. They asked her; "Why do you need salt, why didn't you prepare enough beforehand?" She answered; "I took enough for our own needs, but guests came to us and it is for them that I need salt."

In this manner all the people of Sodom knew that Lot was harbouring guests. While his wife was out, Lot made his guests a feast, and baked unleavened bread, and they ate.

Before they lay down for the night, the men of the city, the men of Sodom, both young and old, from every quarter, surrounded the house; and they called to Lot; "Where are the men who came to you tonight? Bring them out to us, that we may know them." They said this because they desired to rape them. Opening the door, Lot went outside to the men (shutting the door behind him), and said; "I beg you, my brothers, do not commit such a wrong. Look, I have two recently pubescent daughters who have not known man; let me bring them out to you, and do to them as you please; only do nothing to these men, for they have come under the shelter of my roof." (Now a man usually allows himself to be killed in order to save his wife and children, but Lot was willing to allow the townspeople to abuse and gang rape his daughters). But the men of Sodom mocked Lot and said, "Stand back! The fellow came here as an alien, and already he acts the ruler! Now we will deal worse with you than with them." And they pressed hard against the person of Lot, and moved forward to break the door. But the angels put forth their hands and brought Lot into the house to them, and shut the door. They struck with blindness the men who were at the door of the house, both small and great, so that they wearied themselves groping for the door. They said to Lot; "Have you anyone else here? Sons-in-law, sons, daughters, or any one you have in the city, bring them out of the city; for we are about to destroy this place, because the outcry against its people has become great before Yahweh, and Yahweh has sent us to destroy it." So Lot went out and said to his sons-in-law, who were married to two of his daughters; "Up, get out of this place; for Yahweh is about to destroy the city." But he seemed to his sons-in-law to be jesting.

When morning dawned, the angels urged Lot, saying; "Arise, take your wife and your two daughters who are here, lest you be consumed in the punishment of the city."

But Lot did not wish to leave, and so he lingered. The angels seized him and his wife and his two daughters by the hand, because Yahweh was being merciful to him, and they brought him forth and set him outside the city. Once they were brought forth from the city, Raphael said; "Flee for your life; do not look back or stop anywhere in the valley; flee to the hills, lest you be swept away. Do not look behind you, for verily the Shekhinah of Yahweh, blessed be He, has descended in order to rain upon Sodom and upon Gomorrah brimstone and fire." And Lot said to them; "Oh, no, my lords; behold, your servant has found favour in your sight, and you have shown me great kindness in saving my life; but I cannot flee to the hills, lest the disaster overtake me, and I die. But look over there, that city is near enough to flee to, and it is a little one. Let me escape there, (is it not a little one?) and my life will be saved!" Gabriel said to him; "See, I have favoured you concerning this thing also, in that I will not overthrow this city for which you have spoken. Hurry! Escape there! For I cannot do anything until you arrive there." Therefore the name of the city was called Zoar, (which means 'little' or 'insignificant').

The sun had risen by the time Lot came to Zoar. Gabriel rained sulfurous fire from Yahweh out of heaven upon Sodom and Gomorrah. He annihilated those cities and the entire valley, and all the inhabitants of the cities and the vegetation of the ground. Lot's wife was behind him. Pity stirred within Lot's wife for two of her daughters, who were married in Sodom, and for the life she was leaving behind, and she looked back

> Yahweh, bound by His own righteousness and honour, could not bring this judgment on Sodom until the few righteous people were rescued.

behind her to see if they were coming after her or not. And she saw behind the Shekhinah, and became paralysed, unable to go forward. She became a pillar of salt: the very image of tears petrified.

Whilst in Zoar, Lot observed the rise and increase of the waters, that after the inferno had began to overflow the valley, and which, mixing with the ruins, by degrees, was making the Dead Sea. The Dead Sea, with its sulphureous vapour, the great blocks of saltpetre and sulphur which lie on every hand, and the utter absence of the slightest life in its waters, is a striking testimony to this catastrophe. In those waters, Lot concluded, Zoar, though it had escaped the fire, would also end up perishing because it stood upon the same flat. So Lot was afraid to live in Zoar, and decided it was a good idea to head to the mountain that Yahweh had appointed for safety.

Soon after arriving in Zoar, Lot left the valley, and withdrew to the mountains of Moab, and lived in a cave in the hills with his two daughters. The cave in which they lived became a portent of the World to Come, dripping with wine; "And in that day, the mountains shall drip with wine" (Joel 4:18).

Lot secretly lusted after his virgin daughters. He was intoxicated when he lay with the elder sister, but he was sober when she rose. Despite his knowledge of what had transpired, he did not refrain from drinking wine the next night as well, and lying with his younger daughter. He did so until both became pregnant, for a virgin does not usually become pregnant from her first intercourse. The elder of the two bore a son, and called his name Moab; he is the father of the Moabites to this day. The younger also bore a son, and called his name Ben-ammi; he is the father of the Ammonites to this day.

> According to medical reports, the incidence of pregnancy for one-time unprotected sexual intercourse is between 3.1-5%.

Later Jewish hatred towards the Moabites and Ammonites, and the knowledge that though Lot may be a notorious villain and a sordid weakling, he was still the nephew of Abram the patriarch: who was the progenitor of the nation, and hence the noble name and family honour had to be preserved, that led to the shifting of the blame onto the two daughters. It was claimed the elder daughter said to the younger; "Our father is old, and there is not a man on earth to come in to us after the manner of all the earth. Come, let us make our father drink wine, and we will lie with him, that we may preserve offspring from our father." Yet there were plenty of men in the land, specifically in the nearby town of Zoar to which Lot had insisted on going after the Sodom disaster and from which others had headed into the mountains too. Also, about a day's walk away were the tents of the tribe of Lot's uncle, Abram, who was observing the calamitous seismic activity of the destruction of Sodom from the hills surrounding the valley. To blame the daughters, they claimed Lot was too drunk: that he could not have done it, his daughters must have seduced him! So they worded it thus saying; "the daughters made their father drink wine that night. And the elder of the two went in and lay with her father. He did not know when she lay down or when she arose. The next day, she said to the younger; "Behold, I lay last night with my father. Let us make him drink wine tonight also. Then you go in and lie with him, that we may preserve offspring from our father." So they made their father drink wine that night also. And the younger arose and lay with him, and he did not know when she lay down or when she arose. Thus both the daughters of Lot became pregnant by their father."

Yahweh though knew the honest minds and good thoughts of the two girls. Accordingly, when He commanded; "no Ammonite or Moabite shall be admitted into My congregation" (Deut. 23:4), this prohibition against intermarriage applied only to the males, and not to the females. Ruth, a Moabite, was the ancestress of King David and, eventually, of the Messiah, from Ruth's marriage to Boaz.

QUESTIONS TO PONDER

- When reflecting on what you know of the stories of Lot, Sodom and Gomorrah, I wonder what questions the differences in these stories raises for you.

- I wonder how do you react towards Lot's behaviour.

- Reviewing how the different characters behave, what tools of manipulation and abuse can you see?

- Where in this story do you see trauma, and what are its effects?

- I wonder what in this story unsettles you the most.

- I wonder how we can minister to people who have experienced the types of trauma identifiable in this story.

VIOLATION & VENGEANCE

Jacob the patriarch had a daughter with his wife Leah. Her name was Dinah. Jacob moved his family from Paddan-aram and arrived safe in the city of Shechem, which is in the land of Canaan, and encamped before the city. Soon after arriving there, women of the inhabitants of the land went to the city of Shechem to dance and be merry with the daughters of the city people, and Rachel and Leah, (Jacob's wives), with their families went along to witness the festivities of the daughters of the city. Dinah went out of the camp and into the city to visit the daughters of the land. She went to see and learn the manners, customs, and fashions of the women of that country.

She saw the daughters of the city and remained among them while all the people of the city stood around them, to see their rejoicings; and all the prominent citizens were present, and Shechem the son of Hamor, the ruler of the land, was likewise there to see them. And when Shechem saw Dinah sitting with her mother before the daughters of the city, the maiden pleased him greatly and he inquired of his friends and of his people, saying; "Whose daughter is she that sits among the women and whom I do not know in this city?" And they said to him; "that is the daughter of Jacob the Hebrew, who is camped outside the city, and when she heard that the daughters of the land were going to a festival, she also came with her mother and maid-servant to sit amongst them, as you see now." And Shechem continued looking at Dinah, and his soul clave to Dinah. Soon Shechem went, grabbed her, took her and had intercourse with her by force. He oppressed her, offered violence to her, whence he humbled her. At ths point Dinah was between nine and thirteen years old. Shechem's position in the community was the reason that no one came to Dinah's assistance when she cried for help against being raped. Shechem was strongly drawn to the soul of Dinah, and was in love with the maiden, and he spoke to her tenderly. It was in some degree an extenuation of the wickedness of Shechem that he did not cast off the victim of his violence and lust, but continued to regard her with affection. Dinah was now detained in the house of Shechem, so Shechem went and said insistently to his father Hamor; "Get me this girl as a wife." So Hamor, son of Hidekem the Hivite, went into the house of Shechem and sat before him; and Hamor said to his son; "is there not a woman among the daughters of this land worthy to be your wife, that you want to take a Hebrew woman, who is not of your people?" And Shechem replied; "She is the only one which you must get for me, for she pleases me best." And Hamor decided to do the will of his son, for he dearly loved him.

As Dinah did not return Jacob asked the maidservants who had gone out with her about where she was. Jacob heard that the son of Hamor had defiled his daughter Dinah; but since his sons were in the field a considerable distance away with his cattle, Jacob sent a message to them asking them to return home, and kept silent until they returned. He realized that nothing could be accomplished through the ordinary channels of justice, but to apply force he would need the help of his sons. When Hamor noticed that Jacob's reaction had been silence he began to worry about reprisals, and so he came out to Jacob to speak to him.

Meanwhile Jacob's sons, having heard the news of Dinah's rape, came in from the field prematurely and in a hurry. The men were distressed and very angry, because Shechem had committed an outrage in Israel by having intercourse with Jacob's daughter—a thing not to be done. They said; "such a thing must not happen, even to the daughter of common parents, much less one of a distinguished family such as ours."

And Hamor spoke with them, saying; "My son Shechem longs for, and has chosen in his heart your daughter. Please therefore give her to him in marriage to be his wife. Intermarry with us: give your daughters to us, and take our daughters for yourselves. You will dwell among us, and the land will be open before you; settle, move about, trade and acquire holdings in it." Normally, newcomers like Jacob's family, were not allowed to engage in the kind of commerce or artisanship that would compete with that practiced by the local inhabitants.

Then Shechem spoke out imploringly to Dinah's father and brothers; "Do me this favour that I would find grace before you, and I will pay whatever you tell me. Ask of me a bride-price ever so high, go on, multiply your demand, as well as for gifts, and I will pay what you tell me; only give me the maiden for a wife."

Jacob's sons answered Shechem and his father Hamor—speaking with wisdom and guile (because he had defiled their sister Dinah) — and Simeon and Levi said to them; "We cannot do this thing, to give our sister to a man who is uncircumcised, for that is a disgrace among us. Only on this condition will we agree with you; that you will become like us in that every male among you is circumcised. Then we will give our daughters to you and take your daughters to ourselves; and we will dwell among you and become as one kindred. But if you will not listen to us and become circumcised, we will take our daughter and go."

Here the brothers displayed great astuteness. As a rule, swindlers prefer to be very vague when describing the conditions under which they enter into commitments; not only that, but they usually leave the other party many loopholes in order to lure that party into entering into the desired contract. The sons of Jacob reversed this procedure in order to remove any doubt from the people of Shechem that they were being tricked. They offered their daughters in marriage without reservations, and explained that as a result they themselves would marry the local girls.

Their anger had been provoked primarily by Shechem's acts of kidnapping and rape, but they mentioned only his lack of circumcision. This deceived him into thinking that rectifying this would satisfy them and was designed to convince Hamor and his people that their intentions were honourable. Besides which, the sons of Jacob never expected for a moment that Shechem and his father Hamor would agree to this condition to circumcise themselves and all the males in

> On his deathbed, Jacob will curse Simeon and Levi's anger (Genesis 49). Their tribal portions in the land of Israel are to be dispersed so that they would not be able to regroup and fight arbitrarily.

TALES OF TRAUMA | 45

the city merely on account of a young girl! They reasoned that seeing that not all the males in that city would perform circumcision on themselves, they would be free to take their revenge on them. And whilst it was Shechem who had raped Dinah, they would take retribution on the whole city for the city had witnessed the evil act of Shechem kidnapping Dinah and did not judge him. For this Simeon and Levi decided that they deserved to die.

And yet, whilst they did not threaten retaliatory action for the rape of their sister they made clear that they would not be leaving Dinah in Shechem's house should their offer not be acceptable they would take their sister and leave the region. They made it clear that they did feel insulted and that therefore they could not consider remaining in a region where rape went unopposed. On the other hand, if the people were to circumcise themselves en masse this would show a change of heart on their part towards the laws of sexual purity. It was the brothers' astuteness that caused Hamor to tell his people that the family of Jacob were sincere.

Their words pleased Hamor and Hamor's son Shechem. And the youth lost no time in doing the thing, for he wanted Jacob's daughter. Now he was the most respected in his father's house. So Hamor and his son Shechem went to the gate of their city, for the gate was a public place for holding an assembly of the elders of the town together with the other influential citizens as was the custom pertaining to all matters of common concern, and spoke to the men of their city saying;

"These people are our friends, they are at peace with us, (that is to say they do not harbour hatred against us that we should have to be afraid they are out to trick us); let them settle and dwell in the land and move about and trade in it, for the land is large enough for them; we will take their daughters to ourselves as wives and give

our daughters to them. But only on this condition will the men agree with us to dwell among us and be as one kindred: that all our males become circumcised as they are circumcised. And then shall not all their cattle and substance and all their beasts be ours? We only need agree to their terms, so that they will settle among us."

All the people who went into the gate of the city and heard Hamor and his son Shechem, accepted the proposal, and they agreed to be circumcised; for Shechem and his father, Hamor, were highly respected in their eyes, being the princes of the land. No one was allowed to leave the city until after he had been circumcised.

And next morning Shechem and his father, Hamor, rose early and gathered together all the male persons into the middle of the city, and they called the sons of Jacob and they began circumcising every male amongst them. And they circumcised also Shechem and his father, Hamor, with his five brothers, and each of them then returned to his house. All males, all those who went out of the gate of his town, were thus circumcised.

On the third day, when they were in pain, and regretted having agreed to undergo circumcision, Simeon and Levi, two of Jacob's sons, brothers of Dinah, took each his sword, and came upon the city securely and unmolested. The reason they had waited until the third day was that it took the people until that day to complete the process of circumcising all the men and boys. On that day those who had been circumcised on the first day were still suffering from pains and relatively weak. Another reason that they waited till the third day was due to the accepted belief that amongst all creatures the third is always relatively weak. It makes no difference whether it is the third day after a woman has given birth or whether it is the third day in the development of anything else. This is all due to the fact that the third day was under the aegis of the planet Mars. This is why the pain after a wound has been inflicted was always greater on the third day. This is why the pain of circumcision is greatest on the third day, weakening the person who has undergone this procedure.

> A science known as Techunah, (a form of astronomy) wrote that the third day is the day under the influence of the horoscope cancer, which in turn is presided over by Samael. Samael's personal servant is the planet Mars.

And so it was that Simeon and Levi then killed every male inhabitant. They put Hamor and his son Shechem to the sword, took Dinah out of Shechem's house, and went away. The other sons of Jacob came upon the slain and plundered the town, because their sister had been defiled. All of Jacob's sons participated in the looting. They were entitled to do so as they had all suffered humiliation by the rape of their sister. Each one was entitled to take his share. This is why they all assembled there to determine their respective shares of the compensation due them. Although there is a rule that if someone is executed for a crime then one does not exact financial penalties in addition, this rule does not apply to Gentiles. When they determined that the combined wealth of the townspeople was not adequate, they simply carted off all their belongings on behalf of their father to whom all this belonged. They seized their flocks and herds and asses, and all things whatsoever were in the city, and whatsoever were outside; all their wealth, all their children, and their wives, all that was in the houses, they took as captives and booty.

Jacob said to Simeon and Levi; "You have brought trouble on me, making me odious among the inhabitants of the land, the Canaanites and the Perizzites; my men are few in number, so that if they unite against me and attack me, I and my house will be destroyed."

> Jacob saying; "you have brought trouble" has the same meaning as 'troubled waters' i.e. (waters that are disturbed, not clear). A tradition says Jacob said; "the wine in the cask was clear but you have troubled it".

Jacob had thought that they intended to rescue Dinah with their subterfuge and perhaps to kill Shechem as well, not slaughter the entire city. Jacob said to Simeon and Levi; "You have brought trouble on me, making me odious among the inhabitants of the land, the Canaanites and the Perizzites; my men are few in number, so that if they unite against me and attack me, I and my house will be destroyed."

The Canaanites had a tradition that they would fall by the hands of the sons of Jacob, but they thought that this would happen; "when you shall increase, then shall you inherit the land". Consequently they had not attacked them.

But Simeon and Levi answered; "Should he do with our sister as one does with a whore? Only a whore does not have anyone standing up in her defence, avenging violence done to her; shall the people who you are afraid of rising up against us be allowed to get away with such conduct towards one who was not a whore? It is incumbent upon us to avenge her disgrace. Once the inhabitants of the region will understand this, they will have no reason to attack us."

It is also possible that the brothers considered their action as one that would serve notice on the surrounding tribes not to take liberties with their family. Having seen what happened to an individual who used violence against a member of Jacob's family, they would take this to heart and be forewarned of the consequences of such deeds in the future.

An angel said to Jacob in a dream; "Arise, go up to Bethel and remain there; and build an altar there to Yahweh, who had appeared to you when you were fleeing from your brother Esau." So Jacob, his household and to all who were with him, went up to Bethel.

QUESTIONS TO PONDER

- When reflecting on what you know of the story of Dinah, I wonder what questions the differences in these stories raises for you.

- I wonder how do you react towards the treatment of Dinah.

- I wonder how do you react towards the response of Dinah's brothers.

- Reviewing how the different characters behave, what tools of manipulation and abuse can you see?

- Where in this story do you see trauma, and what are its effects?

- I wonder what in this story unsettles you the most.

- I wonder how we can minister to people who have experienced the types of trauma identifiable in this story.

THE DAUGHTER-IN-LAW

A mong the sons of Jacob the patriarch, unity was never a significant force. Soon after Jacob's older sons sold Joseph, their younger brother, into slavery, Judah chose to leave his father and brothers. The sons of Jacob often took their sheep in search of pasture and Hirah had shown Judah hospitality, and friendship had grown between them. So when Judah left his brothers, he went and pitched his tent close by Hirah, who was an Adullamite.

There, Judah saw the daughter of Shua, a Canaanite, and he married her and had intercourse with her. Yahweh said to Judah; "until now you had no sons, and did not experience the grief caused by sons, but since you tormented your father, and deceived him with the words 'Joseph is without doubts torn to pieces', by your life, you shall wed, bury your children, and suffer the grief that comes with children."

Judah's wife conceived and bore a son, and Judah named him Er, because he was to die without a child. Within a short space of time of having given birth to Er, she conceived again and bore another son, and she named him Onan, because his father would have to mourn for him. Very soon thereafter again she bore a son, and named him Shelah; Judah was at Chezib when she bore him.

> Custom had the father name the first child, the mother the second. The father should have named the third son, but seeing that Judah was in Chezib at the time of his birth, Judah's wife named him.

Judah took a wife for Er his firstborn, a daughter of Shem the great, whose name was Tamar. Er was about fifteen at the time. Tamar was beautiful and desired a family. But Judah's wife commanded her son Er to not have children with Tamar because Tamar was not of the daughters of Canaan. Er accepted his mother's directives, but mainly because he did not want Tamar to become pregnant in case it ruined her beauty. Instead Er compelled Tamar to have anal intercourse, and enjoyed having his evil-smelling semen then spill out on the bed sheets. Er, Judah's first-born, was thus displeasing to Yahweh, and Yahweh took his life.

Then Judah said to Onan; "have intercourse with your brother's wife and do your duty by her as a brother-in-law, and provide offspring for your brother." Judah said this because when brothers live together and one of them dies, and has no son, the wife of the deceased shall not be married outside the family to a strange man. Her husband's brother shall have intercourse with her and take her to himself as wife and perform the duty of a husband's brother to her. And it shall be that the first-born whom she bears shall assume the name of his dead brother that his name may not be blotted out. This marriage custom had been a common practice in the Near East and was not initiated by Yahweh.

But Onan realised that any offspring from Tamar would not count as his, and would only further the cause of his deceased brother rather than his own. Consequently, Onan was not willing to have any children by her, and let his sperm spill on the earth and go to waste whenever he had intercourse with his brother's wife, so as not to provide offspring for his brother.

Onan sinned because his motivation was evil. Onan sinned against his father by not following Judah's instruction; against Tamar by using her sexually and doing all he could to prevent her from conceiving; and against Er, his dead brother, by putting his own personal interests above his brother's inability to continue the family line. What he did was displeasing to Yahweh, and He took his life also.

Judah never knew why children had not been conceived. But from Judah's biased perspective it was Tamar who was the one who caused the death of her husbands and was not able to conceive, and this prompted him to withhold his last son. Then Judah

---

Onan reasoned that if he were to impregnate the widow of his brother, then not only would he also destroy his own ancestral share of the land, but be working the land for another. A similar consideration was raised in the Book of Ruth 4:6 when a potential redeemer declined to perform a levirate marriage with Ruth though there, as Ruth was a Moabite and not a Jewess, his consideration was not sinful: 'the redeemer replied; "Then I cannot redeem it for myself, lest I impair my own estate. You take over my right of redemption, for I am unable to exercise it."

---

said to his daughter-in-law Tamar; "Stay as a widow in your father's house until my son Shelah grows up," for he thought Shelah too might die like his brothers. So Tamar went to live in her father's house. This was a rejection of Tamar as Shelah's future wife: Judah had no intention of ever letting Shelah marry Tamar. Henceforth Tamar was to become isolated, lonely, an outcast.

And the days grew long and multiplied, and the daughter of Shuah, Judah's wife, died. When his period of mourning was over, Judah went up to Timnah with his sheepshearers, together with his friend Hirah the Adullamite. And Tamar was told; "Your father-in-law is coming up to Timnah for the sheepshearing." The fact that Judah attended the shearing (a festive occasion), Tamar knew that he had finished mourning. At this point it was proper for Judah to bring his daughter-in-law into his house and give Tamar his wife's quarters to live in. The fact that he did not caused her to despair of having any kind of future in his family. In her society not only were the younger brothers able to raise up offspring to her husband, but also her father-in-law. Now, enough time elapsed for Shelah to come of age. This was around twelve months from the death of Onan. Finally Tamar was convinced that Judah had no intention of giving Shelah to her. Having seen that Shelah was grown up, yet she had not been given to him as wife, if she were to bear children to carry on the name of her first husband, she must force the issue.

She took off her widow's garb, covered her face with a veil, and, wrapping herself up, sat down at the entrance to Enaim, at the beginning of two major roads, which is on the road to Timnah. Tamar wittingly disguised/veiled her face and donned beautiful garments, so that Judah could not recognize her, and knowing Judah very well (moral purity not being one of his virtues) sat down to wait his passing for the sheep-shearing was an occasion of festivity and often of licentiousness.

When Judah saw her, he took her for a harlot; for she had covered her face. So he turned aside to her by the road, his lust towards her being excited at the sight of her; perhaps he left his friend Hirah the Adullamite, and sent him on his way, while he committed the following. He said; "Here, let me have sex with you"—for he did not know that she was his daughter-in-law. "What," she asked, "will you pay for having intercourse with me?"

He replied; "I will send a kid from my flock." But she said; "You must leave a pledge until you have sent it."

And he said; "What pledge shall I give you?" She replied; "Your seal and cord, and the staff which you carry." The seal, cord, and staff were not items purchased from mass-produced stock. Each had distinctive characteristics that were particular to the owner.

The seal was the ancient cylinder seal used in the making of contracts. The staff referred to the staff that princes and dignitaries are in the habit of carrying. It was a hallmark of the authority of the dynasty of Judah when Jacob blessed him before his death.

So Judah gave them to her and had sexual intercourse with her, and she conceived by him.

> The seal was a cylinder with the unique design of its owner carved in it. When a contract was made, hot wax was put on the document and the seal was rolled over it, leaving the impression of the owner of the seal.

Then she went on her way. She took off her veil and again put on her widow's garb.

Judah sent the kid by his friend the Adullamite, to redeem the pledge from the woman; but he could not find her. He inquired of the people of that town; "Where is the cult prostitute, the one at Enaim, by the road?" For the The religion of the Canaanites had prostitution as a part of their worship of the god of fertility. Judah, in his spiritual and moral dullness, was ignorant of such distinctions. To him it was merely an affair, but to the Canaanites it was an act of worship. *But they said; "There has been no prostitute here." So he returned to Judah and said; "I could not find her; moreover, the townspeople said: There has been no prostitute here." Judah said; "Let her keep them, lest we become a laughingstock for yielding up my possessions for such an ignoble purpose. I did send her this kid, but you did not find her."*

About three months later, it was declared to Judah; "Your daughter-in-law Tamar has committed fornication, by being a whore. In fact, she is with child by this." Sooner or later he would have to face the fact that Shelah, his only living son, was pledged to Tamar. If Tamar were put to death, his problem would be solved. *"Bring her out," said Judah; "and let her be burned."* This death penalty, which had been decreed upon Tamar, was a man-made ordinance applicable to certain sexual offences by the Gentiles.

> Because Judah had deceived his father through a kid of the goats — for he had dipped Joseph's coat in its blood — therefore he, too, was deceived through a kid of the goats.

TALES OF TRAUMA | 57

As she was being brought out, she sent this message to her father-in-law; "I am pregnant and with child by the man to whom these belong." And she added; "Examine these: whose seal and cord and staff are these?"

Judah, the forefather of the Messiah and the great-grandson of Abram, recognized them, and had to say of this woman; "She is more in the right than I, inasmuch as I did not give her to my son Shelah." And he was not intimate with her again. He did not sleep with her again as he was ashamed to do so seeing that he was her father-in-law. When the time came for her to give birth, there were twins in her womb! The midwife noticed this before Tamar had commenced giving birth. And so she had a means of identification ready to make sure the firstborn would be identified as such. While she was in labor, one of them put out his hand, and the midwife tied a crimson thread on that hand, to signify: This one came out first.

But then, he drew back his hand, and out came his brother; and she said; "What a breach you have made for yourself!" By this she meant that the hand of the first one indicated that he was about to emerge from the womb before you, his brother, why did you push your way out past him thus blocking him becoming the first-born? The emergence of a whole baby from the mother's birth canal first determines who is the true firstborn. So he was named Perez.

Afterward his brother came out, on whose hand was the crimson thread; he was named Zerah in commemoration of the red string she had wound around his hand.

> Perez, turns out to be the son of Judah who would carry on the messianic line until the time of David, and ultimately, of Jesus (Ruth 4:12; Matthew 1:3).

The kingdom of David stemmed from Peretz whose dynasty symbolised the moon and its ups and downs. The moon's orbit is completed every 29 days. This is why you will find that there were 29 righteous people (descended from him) listed in the Bible from the time of Peretz until the last King of the Davidic dynasty.

QUESTIONS TO PONDER

- When reflecting on what you know of the story of Judah, Tamar, and her husbands, I wonder what questions the differences in these stories raises for you.

- I wonder how do you react towards the treatment of Tamar.

- I wonder how do you react towards the response of Judah.

- Reviewing how the different characters behave, what tools of manipulation and abuse can you see?

- Where in this story do you see trauma, and what are its effects?

- I wonder what in this story unsettles you the most.

- I wonder how we can minister to people who have experienced the types of trauma identifiable in this story.

THE WARRIOR'S VOW

There came a time when the Israelites once more began to do evil in Yahweh's sight. Yair was sitting as judge over the Israelites at the time. They turned to serving Baalim and Astoreth, and worshipping the gods of the Sidonians, the Moabites, the Ammonites, and the gods of the Philistines. As this behaviour grew worse and worse, the Israelites stopped serving Yahweh and, as they turned solely to the idols of the foreign gods, they forsook Yahweh completely.

Yahweh, in anger became incensed with Israel and sold them into the hands of the Philistines and the Ammonites, so that the Israelites were assaulted from both their east and their west sides. This vexation and oppression started during the fourth year of Yairs' judicature, and dominion and continued for eighteen years. Jair could act as judge to determine differences amongst the Israelites, but he could not deliver them from their enemies. In the year Yair died, his twenty-second in office, the Philistines and the Ammonites battered and shattered the Israelites that were on the other side Jordan in what had been the land of the Amorites, which is in Gilead.

The Ammonites also crossed the Jordan to make war on Judah, Benjamin, and the House of Ephraim. Israel was in great distress. It was then that the sons of Israel cried out to Yahweh wailing; "We stand guilty. We have sinned against you: we have forsaken you our God and served also Baalim in preference to you."

But Yahweh said to the Israelites; "I have rescued you from the Egyptians, from the Amorites, from the Ammonites, and from the Philistines. The Sidonians, the Amalekites, and the Midianites also oppressed you; and when you cried out to Me, on that day I delivered you from out of their hand. Yet you have forsaken me and have served other gods. No, I will deliver you no more. Go cry to the gods you have freely chosen over Me: the gods of your oppressors; let them deliver you in your time of distress!"

> The Sidonians were from Sidon, a seaport on the Mediterranean Sea in modern Lebanon. Sidon received its name from the first-born of Canaan, the grandson of Noah (Genesis 10:15, 19). It was also the birthplace of the Phoenician princess Jezebel (1 Kings 16:31)

The sons of Israel responded to Yahweh saying; "We have sinned, so yes, chastise us as you see fit, with your own hand and by your own design, only deliver us this day from our oppressors and do not give us up into the hands of these cruel men!" Then, as evidence of the sincerity of their sorrow, the Israelites gathered up and removed the foreign gods from among them and they served Yahweh again. Yahweh's soul was grieved at their anguish. Yahweh pitied them and could not bear the miseries of Israel.

The Ammonites were called to arms. They came and gathered together, and they encamped in Gilead. The Israelites also assembled themselves together, and they encamped at Mizpah. The troops there, the officers of Gilead, said to each other; "whichever man is willing to be the first to fight the Ammonites will be chieftain over all the inhabitants of Gilead."

Now Jephthah the Gileadite was an able warrior. He was the bastard son of a prostitute. Jephthah's father, Gilead, also had sons by his wife, and when the wife's sons grew up, they drove Jephthah out, saying; "You shall have no share in our father's property, for you are the son of an outsider." So Jephthah fled from his brothers and settled in the land of Tob, near Gilead. Vein men of low character, (who desired to get their living by spoil and rapine rather than through decent labour), gathered about Jephthah and went out raiding with him. When the Ammonites formally went to war against Israel and attacked, the elders of Gilead went to bring Jephthah back from the land of Tob, for he had managed his band of men well: employing them against the enemies that bordered upon them; and

The land of Tob was the name of a place in ancient Israel, but the exact location is not known. It is identified with the region centring on Taibiyah, southeast of the Sea of Galilee, and is probably also the place mentioned in 2 Samuel 10:6-8 as one of the small Syrian Kingdoms that made up Aram.

particularly upon parties of the Ammonites. This is why the elders of Gilead moved forward to choose Jephthah for their chieftain in this war and to be one of their judges. He was chosen for the because of his bravery and might and not because of his Scriptural knowledge or understanding about the commandments of Yahweh; of which he was woefully ignorant.

The elders of Gilead approached Jephthah saying; "Come! be our chief, so that we can fight the Ammonites."

Jephthah replied; "Are you not the very people who hated me and drove me out of my father's house and depriving me of a share in my father's goods, which was my due? How can you come to me now when you are in distress?"

The elders of Gilead responded; "Honestly, we have now turned back to you. If you come with us and fight the Ammonites, you shall be head over all the inhabitants of Gilead."

Jephthah said; "If you recall me from this place where I am now settled and you bring me home again to the place whence I was expelled to fight against the Ammonites, and Yahweh delivers them before me, will you really make good this promise that I shall I be your head?"

And the elders of Gilead answered Jepthah; "Yahweh shall be witness between us: we will do just as you have said." Then Jephthah went with the elders of Gilead, and the people made him head and chief over them. Jephthah repeated all the terms of their agreement before Yahweh and the assembled Israelites at Mizpah.

Jephthah then sent messengers to prevent blood-shed, in order that the Israelites might be acquitted from all the sad consequences of this war, to the king of the Ammonites, saying; "What have you against me that you have come against me to fight in my land?" The king of the Ammonites replied to Jephthah's messengers; "When Israel came from Egypt, they seized the land which is mine, from the Arnon to the Jabbok as far as the Jordan. Now, then, restore it peaceably."

Jephthah again sent messengers to the king of the Ammonites.

He said; "Israel did not seize the land of Moab or the land of the Ammonites. When they left Egypt, Israel travelled through the wilderness to the Red Sea, south of the land of Edom, and went on to Kadesh. Israel then sent messengers to the king of Edom, saying; 'Allow us to cross your country.' But the king of Edom would not consent. They also sent a mission to the kings of Moab and of Moav as well. Both these kings refused. So Israel, after staying peacefully at Kadesh, travelled on through the wilderness, circumventing the land of Edom and the land of Moab. They kept to the east of the land of Moab until they encamped on the other side of the Arnon; and, since Moab ends at the Arnon, they never entered Moabite territory. Then Israel sent messengers to Sihon king of the Amorites, the king of Heshbon. Israel said to him; 'Allow us to cross through your country to our homeland.' But Sihon would not trust Israel to pass through his territory. Sihon mustered all his troops, and they encamped at Jahaz; he engaged Israel in battle. But Yahweh, the God of Israel, delivered Sihon and all his troops into Israel's hands, and they defeated them; and Israel took possession of all the land of the Amorites, the inhabitants of that land: possessing all the territory of the Amorites from the Arnon to the Jabbok and from the wilderness to the Jordan. Now, Yaweh, the God of Israel, dispossessed the Amorites before Israel; should you possess their land? Do you not hold what Chemosh your god gives you to possess? So we will hold on to everything that Yahweh has given to us! Besides, Israel has been inhabiting Heshbon and its dependencies, and Aroer and its dependencies, and all the towns along the Arnon for three hundred years, why have you not tried to recover them all this time? I have done you no wrong; yet you are doing me harm and making war on me. May Yahweh, who judges, determine this controversy by the success of this day and war between the Israelites and the Ammonites!" But the king of the Ammonites paid no heed to the message that Jephthah sent him.

Then the spirit of Yahweh came upon Jephthah. He marched through Gilead and Manasseh, passing Mizpeh of Gilead; and from Mizpeh of Gilead he crossed over the border to the Ammonites. And Jephthah made the following vow to Yahweh; "If you deliver the Ammonites into my hands, then whatever comes out of the door of my house to meet me on my safe return from the Ammonites shall be yours and shall be offered by me as a burnt offering." But as Jephthah made this vow, Yahweh was irritated against him; "What will Jephthah do if an unclean animal comes out to meet him?"

With a great slaughter, Jephthah smote utterly the Ammonites in twenty cities and the plain of the vineyards. The Ammonites submitted to the Israelites.

When Jephthah arrived at his home in Mizpah, behold, there was his daughter coming out to meet him, with timbrels and dances! She was his only child.

On seeing her, he rent his clothes and said; "Alas, my daughter! You have brought me low; you have become one who causes me trouble! For I have made a vow to Yahweh and I cannot retract it, and am indispensably obliged to perform it."

"Father," she said quietly; "you have made a vow to Yahweh; seeing that Yahweh has vindicated you against your enemies, the Ammonites, do to me as you have vowed. Let this be done for me though: let me be alone for two months, and I will go with my companions and lament upon the mountains and there bewail my virginity, — that I shall die childless."

"Go," he replied. He let her go for two months. She and her companions went and bewailed her virginity upon the mountains, for the most important priority that affected women at that time was the necessity of having children.

At the end of the two months she returned to her father, and he did to her as he had vowed: immolating his virgin daughter on the altar. This act was criminal in the sight of Yahweh for a human being cannot be designated as an offering. When Jephthah was on the point of immolating his daughter, she inquired; "Is it written in the Commandments of Yahweh that human beings should be brought as burnt offerings?" Jephthah was an ignorant man who only knew the ways of foreign worship practices, else he would have known that a vow of that kind was not valid: indeed, even if it had been, he merely had to pay a certain sum to the sacred treasury of the Temple in order to be freed from the vow, so he replied; "My daughter, my vow was, whatever comes out of the door of my house to meet me on my safe return from the Ammonites shall be offered by me as a burnt offering.'" She answered; "But Jacob, too, vowed that he would give to Yahweh the tenth part of all that Yahweh gave him. Did he sacrifice any of his sons?" But Jephthah remained inflexible and ignorantly went ahead and offered his daughter as a sacrifice. Had he but consulted with the learned high priest of the time Phinehas, he would have been informed of his error. Jephthah was too arrogant to travel to Phinehas to receive guidance; "I a judge of Israel! Why should I go to him? I will not humiliate myself to my inferior."

> This is reflected greatly in the sentiments of Rachel when she said she would rather die than be barren (Genesis 30:1).

This hubris cost an innocent girl her life. Yahweh punished Jephthah. He became ill, and died by an unnatural decaying of his body. Fragments of flesh fell from his bones at intervals, and were buried where they fell, so that his body was buried in the cities of Gilead.

Jephthah's daughter had never known a man. So it became a custom in Israel for the maidens of Israel to go every year for four days in the year, into the mountains, and chant dirges for the daughter of Jephthah the Gileadite.

This sad ending has been upsetting to people throughout history. So some say that instead of being immolated on an alter she was walled up and had to live the rest of her life in seclusion, and that she was able to only see and speak to people on the four days in the year when the maidens of Israel visited the mountains.

When the Israelites were about to enter the land promised to them by Yahweh, Moses had told the people to be careful not to adopt the ways of foreign worship that were practiced in the region; "You must not worship Yahweh in their way, because in worshiping their gods, they do all kinds of detestable things that Yahweh hates. They even burn their sons and daughters in the fire as sacrifices to their gods." Deut. 12:30-31

QUESTIONS TO PONDER

- When reflecting on what you know of the story of Jephthah. I wonder what questions the differences in these stories raises for you.

- I wonder how do you react towards the treatment of the daughter.

- I wonder how do you react towards the way people responded and lived out religious identity and practice, and what this tells us about knowing our faith and God.

- Reviewing how the different characters behave, what tools of manipulation and abuse can you see?

- Where in this story do you see trauma, and what are its effects?

- I wonder what in this story unsettles you the most.

- I wonder how we can minister to people who have experienced the types of trauma identifiable in this story.

THE LEVITE'S CONCUBINE

In those days, when there was no king in Israel, and the Ark of God's Covenant was there and Phinehas son of Eleazar, son of Aaron the priest, ministered before Yahweh, a Levite man, residing on the side of Mount Ephraim; in a city that was at the other end of the hill country, took to himself a concubine from Bethlehem in Judah.

One day though, the woman, his concubine, became both fearful and angry with her husband and deserted him because he was selfish: putting his comfort before her and their relationship. Leaving, she went to her father's house in Bethlehem in Judah; and she stayed there a full four months.

Then her husband set out, with an attendant and a pair of donkeys, and went after her to woo her and to win her back. She admitted him into her father's house; and when the girl's father saw him, he received him warmly. His father-in-law, the girl's father, pressed him to stay, and so he remained with him three days; so they ate and drank, and lodged there.

He arose early in the morning of the fourth day and prepared to go; but the girl's father said to his son-in-law; "Eat something to give you strength, and then, afterwards you can leave and go on your way." So the two men sat down and they feasted together: eating and drinking. Then the girl's father said; "Won't you stay overnight and enjoy yourself?" When the man got up to go and started to leave, his father-in-law kept urging him until he turned back and spent the night there again. Early in the morning of his fifth day, the man was again about to leave, when the girl's father said; "Come, have a bite to eat that the food may fortify you." So they lingered and the two of them ate and drank: dawdling until past noon while the day declined.

The man, together with his concubine and servant rose to depart. Seeing this, his father-in-law, said to him; "Look, now the day has weakened and it is almost evening. So stop for the night: see it is now the time of day for encamping. Spend the night here and enjoy yourself and arise early tomorrow to start your journey homewards."

But the man did not want to stay the night and refused the invitation. He set out with a team of saddled donkeys, his servant, and concubine, and they travelled as far as the vicinity of Jebus, that is, a district within Jerusalem. They were near Jebus as the sun descended and the day far spent, when the servant said to the man, his master; "Come now, let us turn aside to this town of the Jebusites, and spend the night in it."

But the man replied to his servant; "We will not turn aside to a town of foreigners, who are not of the people of Israel, but instead come, let us approach Gibeah or Ramah and spend the night in either of those places."

So they travelled on and went their way, and the sun set when they were near Gibeah, which belonged to Benjamin. So they turned off there and went in to spend the night in Gibeah. He went and sat down in the town square, but nobody took them into their home to spend the night. In the evening, an old man came along from his property in the fields outside the town.

This old man was from the hill country of Ephraim and resided in Gibeah, where the people of the area were Benjaminites. When the old man looked up he happened to see the wayfaring man in the town square. "Where," the old man inquired, "are you going to, and where do you come from?"

He answered the old man; "We are travelling from Bethlehem of Judah to the edge of the mountain of Ephraim. That is where I live. I made a journey to Bethlehem of Judah, and now I am on my way to Shiloh, to the House of Yahweh, berfore returning home. Nobody has taken me into their house. We have both bruised straw and feed for our donkeys, with bread and wine for me and the woman and the young man along with us. We are lacking nothing more than a place to spend the night."

"Peace be to you," said the old man; "Let me take care of all your needs; only do not on any account spend the night in the square." So the old man brought them into his house, and fed produce to the donkeys; then they bathed their feet and ate and drank.

While they were enjoying themselves at the old man's house the men of the town, (a depraved lot), surrounded the house, and began beating on the door. They called to the old man; "Bring out the man who has come into your house, so that we can have intercourse with him."

The old man went out and said to them; "Please, my brothers, do not commit such a wicked act. Since this man has entered my house and is my guest, do not commit this crime. Look, here is my virgin daughter, and his concubine. Let me bring them out to you. Have your pleasure of them, do what you like with them; but do not commit this vile thing to this man."

Though the old man tried reasoning with them, the men would not listen to him. To spare himself, the man seized his concubine and pushed her out to them. They wantonly gang-raped her and abused her all night long until the morning. As the dawn began to break, they let her go. As morning appeared and the sky lightened, the woman came back and collapsed at the entrance of the old man's house where her husband was.

> In the eyes of the Levite man, the concubine had already caused him a degree of humiliation in her act of leaving. As he was now in danger of becoming more humiliated and emasculated by the depraved men, he chose not to be humiliated again. Instead of standing up against the depraved men, in a selfish act designed to keep his own dignity he throws her out himself!

When her husband arose in the morning, he opened the doors of the house and went out to continue his journey. There, outside, with

TALES OF TRAUMA | 73

her hands on the threshold, lying at the entrance of the house where she had fallen, was his concubine.

"Get up," he said to her callously; "we are going." But there was no answer, for she was dead. The man then picked the concubine up and put her on the donkey and the man then set out for his home.

When he got home, he took a knife, and grasping his concubine, he cut her up, limb by limb, into twelve pieces. The Levite man then sent her limbs throughout all the territory of Israel.

All who saw it were shocked and cried out saying; "Never has such a thing ever happened before, or been seen from the day the Israelites came up out of the land of Egypt to this day! Consider it, take counsel, and speak out.'"

Then all the Israelites came together: from Dan to Beer-sheba and even from the land of Gilead. They came forth, and the community assembled as one body before the Lord at Mizpah. All the leaders of the people of all the tribes of Israel presented themselves in the assembly of the people of God. There were 400,000 foot-soldiers bearing arms.

The Israelites said, "Tell us, how did this evil and criminal thing come about?" And the Levite man, the husband of the murdered woman, answered;

"My concubine and I came to Gibeah of Benjamin to spend the night. The men of Gibeah set out to harm me and during the night they surrounded the house. They meant to kill me, and they raped my concubine until she died. So I took hold of my concubine and I cut her into pieces, and sent her throughout all the teritory of Israel; for they have committed an outrageous vile act of depravity in Israel. You are all Israelites; give your advice and counsel and produce a plan of action here and now!"

Then all the people arose as one, declaring; "We will not go back to our tents, and nor will any of us enter our houses! But now this is what we will do to Gibeah: we will wage war against it according to lot. We will take ten men to the hundred, a hundred to the thousand, and a thousand to the ten thousand from all the tribes of Israel, to bring provisions for the troops, to prepare for their going to Gibeah of Benjamin, to repay for all the outrage and disgrace it has committ ed in Israel." So all the men of Israel, united as one, gathered against the town. The tribes of Israel sent men through and to the whole tribe of Benjamin, saying; "What is this crime, this evil thing, that has happened among you? Come, hand over those scoundrels in Gibeah so that we may put them to death and purge from Israel this evil that needs to be stamped out." But the Benjaminites, heard that the people of Israel had gone up to Mizpah, would not listen, nor

---

When Jacob fled, with all his pocessions, wives and children, from the house of Laban, (his father-in-law), Laban discovered this and pursued Jacob. Laban was not happy they had left, but conceded that his daughters had left voluntarily. He agreed to let Jacob go in peace, with Jacob promising to never abuse his daughters or take additional wives (Genesis 31:50). The two men then erected a pile of stones, a metaphoric 'watchtower', called a mizpah, to commemorate this promise. They held God to be their witness. Both also agreed that they would consider the mizpah a border between their respective territories, and would not pass the watchtower to do evil to the other.

yield to the demand of their fellow Israelites. Istead, the Benjaminites gathered together from their towns and came to Gibeah in order to do battle against the Israelites.

On that day, apart from the inhabitants of Gibeah, the Benjaminites mustered 26,000 armed men from their towns; 700 picked men of all this force were left-handed with shriveled right arms, and each of these could sling a stone at a strand of hair and not miss. And the Israelites, other than Benjamin, mustered 400,000 fighting men, all warriors.

The Israelites proceeded to Bethel, and there they inquired of Yahweh; "who of us shall advance first to battle against the Benjaminites?" And the Yahweh replied; "Judah shall." But they did not think as to try inquiring as whether they would be victorious or vanquished. In the morning, the Israelites arose and encamped against Gibeah. There, the men of Israel took the field against the Benjaminites and drew up the battle line. But the Benjaminites issued out of Gibeah, and that day in battle they struck down 22,000 Israelite men. The Israelites went up and wept before Yahweh until the evening and they asked; "Shall we again do battle against our kinsfolk the Benjaminites?" And Yahweh replied; "Go, march against them." So the army of the men of Israel rallied, and again drew up in battle order at the same place as they had on the first day. The Israelites advanced against the Benjaminites on the second day. The Benjaminites came out from Gibeah on the second day and struck down 18,000 of the Israelites. Then all the Israelite army went back up to Bethel and they sat there, weeping and fasting before Yahweh until evening. In the evening they presented burnt offerings and offerings of well-being. The Israelites inquired; "Shall we again take the field against our kinsmen the Benjaminites, or shall we desist?" Yahweh answered; "Go up, for tomorrow I will deliver them into your hands."

So Israel stationed men in ambush on all sides of Gibeah. On the third day, as on the previous two, the Israelites went up against the Benjaminites, and engaged them in battle at Gibeah. When the Benjaminites dashed out to meet the Israelite army, they were drawn away from the town and onto the roads, of which one runs to Bethel and the other to Gibeah, and into the open field. As before, they started to inflict casualties on the Israelite troops, killing about 30 men of Israel.

The Benjaminites thought; "just like previously, the men of Israel are being routed before us!" But the Israelites had planned this attack in advance and thinking; "We will start battling and then retreat, taking flight and drawing them onto the roads and away from the town."

While the main body of the Israelites moved away from their positions and had drawn up its battle line at Baal-tamar, the Israelites, who were waiting in ambush, rushed out from there position at Maareh-geba, (a narrow pass: the 'nakedness' (maareh) was an exposed overlook of Geva Binyamin. It is an uncovered part that was defenceless against conquest), the plain of Geba. Thus 10,000 picked men out of all Israel came to a point south of Gibeah, and the battle was fierce. But the Benjaminites did *not realize that disaster was fast approaching upon them. Yahweh defeated the Benjaminites before Israel and that day the Israelites slew 25,100 men of Benjamin. It was only then that the Benjaminites realized that they were routed. The Israelites had yielded ground to the Benjaminites, because they trusted the troops that they had stationed in ambush against Gibeah. The troops in ambush rushed quickly upon Gibeah. Then they put the whole city to the sword. At the outset, a signal was arranged and agreed between the Israelites and the ambushers, whereby the ambushers would raise continuous smoke from the city. The agreement was that when the ambushers sent up a huge column of smoke out of the town, the main body of Israel should turn in battle, for by his sign the main body of the Israelite army would understand that the ambushers had conquered Gibeah. It was at this point that the Benjaminites had begun to inflict the 30 casualties on the Israelites, and thought; "Surely they are defeated before us, as in the other two battles." But when the cloud, a column of smoke, began to rise out of the town, the Benjaminites looked behind them. They saw the whole town going up in smoke towards the sky! At this, the main body of the Israelite army turned about, and the Benjaminites were dismayed and thrown into a panic, for they realized that disaster had overtaken them. Therefore they turned away and retreated from the Israelites along the road to the wilderness; but fighting caught up with them and the battle overtook them, and those Israelite ambushers who came out of the town were slaughtering them in between; surrounding and cutting down the Benjaminites. They pursued them, and trod them down from Menuhah, their resting place, to a point opposite Gibeah on the east. That day 18,000 men of Benjamin fell. They turned and fled to the wilderness, to the Rock of Rimmon; but the Israelites picked off another 5,000 on the roads and, continued in hot pursuit of them up to Gidom, and there 2,000 more of them were slain. Thus the total number of Benjaminites who fell that day came to 25,000 fighting men, all of them brave.*

However, 600 Benjaminite men had turned and fled to the wilderness, to the Rock of Rimmon. They remained there for four months. Meanwhile, the Israelites turned back to the rest of the Benjaminites, and put them to the sword: towns, people, and animals. Everything that remained. Finally, they set fire to all the towns that were left.

Now the men of Israel, while at Mizpah, had sworn an oath; "None of us will give his daughter in marriage to a Benjaminite." And the people came to Bethel, and sat there until evening before Yahweh, and they lifted up their voices and wept bitterly. The Israelites relented toward their kinsmen the Benjaminites, and they said, "This day one tribe has been cut off from Israel! They cried; "Yahweh, you are the God of Israel. Why has it come to pass that today that one tribe must be missing from Israel?" Early the next day, the people built an altar and brought burnt offerings and offerings of well-being. "What can we do to provide wives for those Benjaminites who are left, seeing that we have sworn to Yahweh not to give any of our daughters to them in marriage?" Thinking hard, the Israelites asked each other; "Is there anyone from all the tribes of Israel who failed to come up to the assembly before Yahweh at Mizpah?" They asked this because a solemn oath had been taken concerning anyone who did not go and that was they were to be put to death. It turned out that when the roll of the troops was taken, no one from Jabesh-gilead had come to the assembly. So the assemblage dispatched 12,000 of the warriors, to Jabesh-gilead and commanded them; "Go, put the inhabitants of Jabesh-gilead to the sword, including the women and the little ones. This is what you are to do: Proscribe to death every man, and every woman who has known a man carnally." And they found among the inhabitants of Jabesh-gilead four hundred young virgins who had not known a man carnally and brought them to the camp at Shiloh, which is in the land of Canaan; that is, west of the Jordan. Then the whole community sent word to the Benjaminites who were at the Rock of Rimmon, and proclaimed peace to them. At this news, the Benjaminites returned. The Israelites gave them the 400 girls who had been spared from the women of Jabesh-gilead. But there were not enough of them to go round.

The people had compassion on Benjamin because Yahweh had made a breach in the tribes of Israel. So the elders asked; "What can we do about wives for those who are left, since the women of Benjamin have been killed off?" Some of the elders argued that; "There must be heirs for the remnant of Benjamin, that a tribe may not be blotted out of Israel: for the survivors must inherit the ancestral property. We cannot give them any of our daughters as wives for we have sworn under oath; 'cursed be anyone who gives a wife to Benjamin!' The tribe's ancestral property remains unclaimed; let us devise a plan whereby they may father children, so that the property will fall into the possession of the remaining survivors, and a tribe will not be obliterated from Israel." The elders came to an agreement.

They spoke to the Benjaminites and instructed them. They said; "Look, the annual feast of Yahweh is taking place at Shiloh, which lies north of Bethel, east of the highway that runs from Bethel to Shechem, and south of Lebonah. Go and lie in wait in the vineyards. Watch, and as soon as you see the girls of Shiloh coming out to join in the dances, then come out from the vineyards and each of you seize a wife from among the girls of Shiloh, and go off for the land of Benjamin. And do not worry, for if their fathers or brothers come and complain to us, we shall say to them; 'Be generous to them for our sake and allow us to have them! We were merciful with them because they did not know what to do. We could not provide each of these men with wives because we did not capture in battle a wife for each man at the time of the war with Jabesh-gilead: except for four hundred of them, and you would *have incurred guilt, and would now be blameworthy, if you yourselves had given your daughters to them as wives."'*

So the Benjaminites did as the elders instructed. They took wives for each of them from the dancers whom they abducted. Then they went and returned to their own territory, and rebuilt their towns and settled in them. So the Israelites departed from there, each to his own tribe and clan; and they all went out from there back to their own territories.

In those days there was no king in Israel; all the people did what was right in their own eyes.

QUESTIONS TO PONDER

- When reflecting on what you know of the story of the Levite man and the Concubine, I wonder what questions the differences in these stories raises for you.

- I wonder how do you react towards the treatment of the concubine.

- I wonder how do you react towards the responses of the Levite man, the Israelites and the Benjaminites.

- Reviewing how the different characters behave, what tools of manipulation and abuse can you see?

- Where in this story do you see trauma, and what are its effects?

- I wonder what in this story unsettles you the most.

- I wonder how we can minister to people who have experienced the types of trauma identifiable in this story.

THE DAUGHTER OF A KING

T hese events happened sometime after King David had attacked Rabbah of Ammon and captured the royal city. His son, Absalom, had a beautiful, intellignet and moral sister named Tamar. This brother and sister were the children of King David through his wife Maacah, who was the daughter of Talmai, king of Geshur. The Crown-prince Amnon, (also a son of King David, born from his wife Ahinoam the Jezreelitess) became infatuated with her; even though she was his half-sister.

Amnon was not used to being refused something he wanted. He was so distraught because of his half-sister Tamar that he became sick; for she was a virgin, and it seemed impossible to Amnon to do anything to her, for Tamar was safely out of Amnon's reach. As a royal princess, and a virgin, she was closely watched by the harem eunuchs.

She lived in the women's quarters, and could not go outside its walls unless accompanied by other women and guards. There seemed no opportunity for Amnon to get her alone, let alone into his bedroom like he desired.

Amnon had a friend named Jonadab, the son of King David's brother Shimah. Jonadab was a very clever man. He asked Amnon; "Why are you so dejected, O prince, morning after morning? Tell me!" Amnon replied; "I am suffering with pining sickness for Tamar, the sister of my brother Absalom!" Amnon discussed his obsession with Tamar to Jonadab. Jonadab then came up with a plan to aide his friend.

Jonadab said to him; "Lie down in your bed and pretend that you are sick. When your father comes to see you, say to him; 'Let my sister Tamar come and give me something to eat. Let her prepare the food in front of me, so that I may look on, and let her serve it to me.'" Jonadab didn't need to add; "and then force yourself on Tamar," because they shared the same wicked thoughts. Jonadab knew that Yahweh looked favourably on those who visited the sick and spared them from the judgment of Gehenna, so this plan of his would gain the support of King David, who had himself written in a psalm; "Happy is the one that considers those who are ill; Yahweh will deliver them in the day of evil".

So Amnon lay down and pretended to be sick. The king, as expected, came to see him, and Amnon said to the king; "Oh Father, my King! Please let my sister Tamar come and prepare a couple of dumplings in front of me, and let her bring them to me."

King David sent a message to Tamar in the palace; "Please go to the house of your brother Amnon and prepare some food for him."

Tamar went to the house of her brother Amnon, who was in bed. She made a paste of flour, mixing it first into boiling water and then afterwards in oil. She then took this dough and kneaded it into dumplings in front of him, and cooked them. She took the pan and set out the food before him, but Amnon, pretending to be petulant and out of sorts, refused to eat. In a seeming fit of temper Amnon then ordered everyone to withdraw out of the room!

King David's heir was not someone to be crossed, and because he seemed ill and cranky, his servants obeyed. This order from the prince also applied to the servants with Tamar. Since they were directly commanded to go, her servants also had to leave the room. After everyone had withdrawn, and still feigning the irritation of a sick person, Amnon went into the bedroom alcove, flung himself onto his bedding and, insisting that he would only eat the food if she brought it to him there and fed him with her own hand, called to Tamar; "Bring the food inside and feed me!" Tamar took the dumplings she had made and brought them to her brother inside.

But when she leant forward with the food to serve them to him, he caught hold of her, pulled her to him, and said to her with feerish urgency; "Come lie with me, sister." But she said to him

TALES OF TRAUMA | 85

strongly; "NO! Don't, brother. Don't force me. Such things are not done in Israel! Don't do such a vile thing!

Where will I carry my shame? And you, you will be like any of the scoundrels in Israel! Please, speak to the king; he will not refuse me to you."

Tamar was struggling for her life, not just her virginity. She knew the Law of Moses commanded against any marriage between a half-brother and half-sister, but said this as a ploy to get away from Amnon. Alone and unguarded, she had no chance of fending him off. She resisted him as best she could, she argued and pleaded, pointed out that what he was doing was wrong, that they could marry if he wished, that rape would bring ruin to them both. If she, especially a princess, were no longer a virgin, then none would want her: even though she was the king's daughter no one would marry her.

But her pleading had no effect on Amnon and he would no listen to her. He was too strong for her; he overpowered her and lay with her by force. He raped her.

Then Amnon felt a very great loathing and hatred for her; indeed, his loathing for her was greater than the passion he had felt for her. Some say that in cases of being driven by lust, a man is even willing to rape a woman to satisfy his evil impulse. Such an act is motivated by sheer lust and completely devoid of love. When he comes back to his senses, he will hate his victim, for once sobriety returns, the rapist realizes that he still feels hollow and depressed, and so their is guilt over their sin. But instead of loathing himself, he projects his loathing onto the woman he raped. Tamar was simply a reminder of his foolish sin. He wanted every reminder of his sin to be put far away.

Some though, say that Amnon's intense hatred came from the fact that while he raped her, one of her public hairs became tied around his penis and caused him to be one whose penis has been severed.

And Amnon looked at her distainfully and said to her with a snarl; "Get out!"

She pleaded with him; "Please don't commit this wrong; to send me away would be even worse than the first wrong you committed against me." If Amnon chose to, he could still redeem, somewhat, the situation by either marrying her or paying her bride-price.

But once again her pleading had no effect on Amnon and he would no listen to her. He summoned his young attendant and said; "Get that woman out of my presence, and bar the door behind her."—

She was wearing an ornamented robe which extended all the way down to the wrists and ankles, for maiden princesses were customarily dressed in such garments.— His attendant took her outside and barred the door after her.

Tamar put dust on her head and rent the ornamented robe she was wearing; she put her hands on her head, and walked away, screaming loudly as she went. Tamar knew, and treated, this event as a calamity. She did not hide the truth that a terrible crime was committed against her and did not succumb to the voice that says; "This was somehow your fault."

Her brother Absalom said to her; "Was it your brother, Amnon, who did this to you? For the present, sister, keep quiet about it; he is your brother. Don't brood over the matter." And Tamar remained in her brother Absalom's house, forlorn.

When King David heard about all this, he was greatly upset, but he did not rebuke his son Amnon, for he favoured him, since he was his first-born. Absalom did not utter a word to Amnon, good or bad; but Absalom hated Amnon because he had raped his sister Tamar.

Two years later, when Absalom was having his flocks sheared at Baal-hazor near Ephraim, Absalom invited all the king's sons. Absalom gave his attendants the following order; "Watch, and when Amnon is intoxicated from drinknig too much wine and I tell you to strike down Amnon, kill him! Don't be afraid, for it is I who give you the order. Act with determination, like brave men!"

Absalom came before king David saying; "Your servant is having his flocks sheared. Would Your Majesty and your retinue accompany your servant?"

But the king answered; "No, my son. We must not all come, or we'll be a burden to you." Absalom urged him, but the King would not come along, and he said good-bye. Thereupon Absalom said; "In that case, let my brother Amnon come with us," to which the king replied;

"He shall not go with you." But Absalom urged him, and he sent with him Amnon and all the other princes.

When Amnon was is intoxicated from drinknig too much wine Absalom's attendants did to as they had been ordered. At this action all the other princes mounted their mules and fled. They were still on the road when a rumour reached David that Absalom had killed all the princes, and that not one of them had survived. At this, David rent his garment and lay down on the ground, and all his courtiers stood by with their clothes rent.

But Jonadab said; "My lord must not think that all the young princes have been killed. Only Amnon is dead; for this has been decided by Absalom ever since his sister Tamar was raped. So only Amnon is dead." The watchman on duty looked up and saw a large crowd coming from the road to his rear, from the side of the hill. Jonadab said to the king; "See, the princes have come! It is just as your servant said." The princes came in and broke down crying. King David and his courtiers wept bitterly, too.

Absalom fled. He came to Talmai son of Ammihud, king of Geshur and remained there three years. And King David mourned over his son a long time.

QUESTIONS TO PONDER

- When reflecting on what you know of the story of Amnon and Tamar, I wonder what questions the differences in these stories raises for you.

- I wonder how do you react towards the treatment of the Tamar.

- I wonder how do you react towards the responses of Tamar's brothers, Kind David, and Jonadab.

- Reviewing how the different characters behave, what tools of manipulation and abuse can you see?

- Where in this story do you see trauma, and what are its effects?

- I wonder what in this story unsettles you the most.

- I wonder how we can minister to people who have experienced the types of trauma identifiable in this story.

THE LITTLE CHILDREN AND THE SHE BEARS

Y*ahweh sent a fiery chariot with fiery horses to bring Elijah up into the heavens. They appeared suddenly and separated him from Elisha, his companion, and Elijah went up to heaven in a whirlwind.*

Elisha reached down and picked up the mantle that had dropped from Elijah. The mantle did not fall from heaven and rest on his shoulders; he had to decide to pick it up and put it on. He struck the water with it and said; "Where is Yahweh, the God of Elijah?" As he struck the water, it parted to the right and to the left, and Elisha crossed over. When the disciples of the prophets at Jericho saw him from a distance, they exclaimed; "The spirit of Elijah has settled on Elisha!"

They went to meet him and bowed low to the ground before him. They said to him; "Did you know that today Yahweh was taking your master? Your servants have fifty able men with them. We do not know where Elijah is, but let us send them to go and look for your master; perhaps the spirit of Yahweh has carried him off and cast him upon some mountain or into some valley." They said this as they thought Yahweh had taken Elijah away to some remote location for a period of time. This was not an unusual occurrence.

Elisha replied; "Do not send them," and he delayed them considerably from sending out people to search for Elijah.

But they kept pressing Elisha for a long time, until he was ashamed to the point of embarrassment and said sadly; "Send them then." He was ashamed and embarrassed as he worried that they might say that he did not want to go to meet his teacher and that he wanted Elijah to stay away so that he could keep his newly acquired position of leadership. They sent out fifty men, who searched for three days but did not find him.

> Elijah was carried into the heavens where his body remained whole and unharmed. He remains hidden from the human world except when he is sent on special missions or to appear to the righteous.

They came back to him while he was still in Jericho; and he said to them; "I told you not to go."

The men of the town said to Elisha; "Look, the town is a pleasant place to live in, as my lord can see; but the water is bad and the land causes bereavement."

Evil had come to the waters due to the wickedness of the residents, and it was the bad waters which caused the ground to be a source of bereavement. The waters had caused many miscarriages for those who drank from them. Some believed Jericho was cursed because Joshua *had cursed it saying; "Cursed of Yahweh be the one who undertakes to fortify Jericho: he shall lay its foundations at the cost of his firstborn, and set up its gates at the cost of his youngest." Elijah then added his own curse when the two sons of Hiel the Bethelite (who fortified Jericho in the reign of King Ahab) died. Hiel had indeed offered his sons as foundation sacrifices: he had laid the foundations of the fortification od Jericho at the cost of his firstborn son Abiram, and set up its door leaves at the cost of his younger son Segub.*

Elisha responded; "Bring me a new dish and put salt in it." They brought it to him. He went to the spring, which was the source of the water, and threw salt into it. And he said; "Thus said Yahweh: I heal this water; no longer shall death and bereavement come from it!" The water has remained wholesome to this day, in accordance with the word spoken by Elisha.

From there Elisha went up to Bethel and as he was going up by the way, there came forth little children out of the city, who mocked him; "Go away, baldy! Go away, baldy!" And said to him; "Go away from here, for you have made the place bald for us, for until now we would be hired to bring sweet water from a distance, and we would earn our livelihood. But when the water became sweet, we have lost our livelihood. Go up, baldy! Go up, baldy like Elijah did!" It is a wicked thing to reproach a person for their natural infirmities or deformities for it adds affliction to the afflicted. But as it was his character as a prophet that they designed to taunt, it bruised his dignity, as Elisha felt that the honour Yahweh had shown by making him a prophet should have been sufficient to cover his baldhead and protect him from their scoffing and jeering. They bade him 'go up like Elijah did', as a further taunt: 'if your master has gone up and if you too are a prophet, why did you not go after him? Where is the fiery chariot? When shall we be rid of you too?'

> A bear's whelp is born with a very thick amniotic sack. It takes much care, labour and difficulty to bring it into this world; more so than any other animal. So much so, that when a bear loses a cub it experiences greater anguish and loss.

Elisha heard their taunts, but anger was kindled within him, so Elisha turned back, and looked on them with a grave and severe look and he determined to himself that he saw in them the malice and evil spirit of their parents and kindred. Believing that authority must be maintained by a firm severity he cursed them in the name of Yahweh, even though it is not proper that Yahweh's name be associated with evil and curses. And suddenly, there came forth out of the adjacent wood two she bears who had been robbed of their whelps and wound up with an extraordinary fury, and the two she bears mauled forty-two of the children. This was a very extraordinary and awful punishment for their wickedness, which they knowingly and willingly committed.

Elisha arrived at Bethel and cared not about any possible revenge of the bereaved parents. He went on from there to Mount Carmel, and from here he returned to Samaria.

94 | THE LITTLE CHILDREN AND THE SHE BEARS

QUESTIONS TO PONDER

- When reflecting on what you know of the story of Elisha and the children, I wonder what questions the story raises for you.

- I wonder how do you react towards the treatment of the children.

- I wonder how do you react towards the responses of religious leaders today in their treatment towards children.

- Reviewing how the different characters behave, what tools of manipulation and abuse can you see?

- Where in this story do you see trauma, and what are its effects?

- I wonder what in this story unsettles you the most.

- I wonder how we can minister to people who have experienced the types of trauma identifiable in this story.

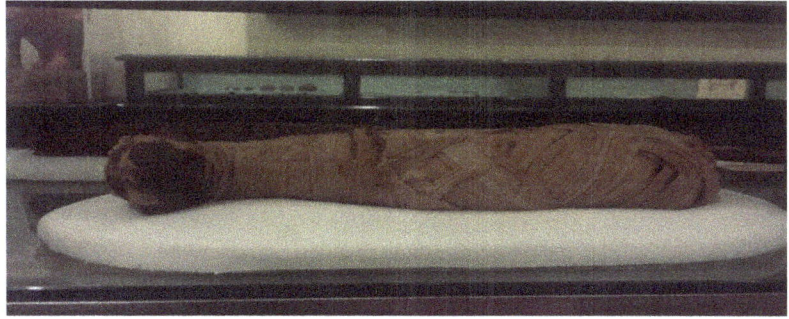

CANNIBAL

B en-Hadad, the king of Aram, that is Damascus, was at war with Jehoram: the ninth king of the northern Kingdom of Israel (he was the son of Ahab and Jezebel).

Ben-Hadad consulted with his officers over a great many wine jars and afterwards he said; "We will dig ditches and I will set up my camp in such and such a place". (This was said in order to conceal and keep secret the location). "I will make my camp. There I will encamp and ambush the king of Israel or his bands of soldiers who pass to plunder in my land through that place."

Elisha the Prophet sent word to the king of Israel; "Beware of passing that place, because the Arameans are going down there and have set an ambush." So the king of Israel sent out his scouts and checked on the place indicated by Elisha.

Finding this to be true, the king of Israel sent word to his men about the place Elisha had told him. Ben-Hadad would move the location of the ambushes, but time and again Elisha would warn the king, so that he was on his guard in such places and took precautions there. When Israel passed by once and twice without falling, Ben-Hadad took notice and beame greatly agitated about the matter, and sent his servant to summon his officers. The king of Aram then demanded of them; "Tell me! Who of us is on the side of the king of Israel?"

> Yahweh revealed the fact that nature has inherent shortcomings. This was as a warning so that people not to take their existence for granted, but being thus forewarned are on guard against evil urges. Once warned, those who fail to heed the warning, become a wicked person. They will suffer death of the soul, which is worse than death of the body. Death of the body is, after all, a fate common to all living creatures regardless of their moral standing. Death of the soul, however, is the result of free choice.

"No one, my lord king," said one of the officers, (believing them all true and faithful); "But it is Elisha, that prophet who is in Israel, that tells Jehoram the very words you speak in your bedroom: the most private place, and in the most secret manner."

Ben-Hadad ordered them saying; "Go then, and find out where he is, so I can send men and capture him. Do not kill him!" The report came back: "He is in Dothan." Dothan had been the place where the sons of Jacob had moved their sheep and, at the suggestion of Judah, had sold their brother Joseph to the Ishmaelite merchants. Ben-Hadad sent his men to invite Elisha to his court in the hope of winning him over. He sent horses and chariots and a strong force there. They went by night and surrounded the city. When Elisha's servant arose and went out early the next morning he saw that an army with horses and chariots had surrounded the city. Elisha's assistant panicked and cried to Elisha; "Oh no, my lord! What shall we do?" But Elisha reassured him, responding; "Do not fear, for there are more with us than with them". Elisha revealed the phalanx of angels that served to protect them. Elisha prayed; "Open his eyes, Yahweh, so that he may see." Then Yahweh opened the servant's eyes, and he saw the reality that he could not see before. He looked and saw the hills full of horses and chariots of fire all around Elisha and that there really were more with, than those against them!

As the enemy came down toward him, Elisha prayed again to Yahweh; "Please strike this army with blindness." As this was a curse it was proper that he did not use Yahweh's name. Yahweh struck them with blindness as Elisha had asked. During the war between Aram and Israel, Yahweh never struck Ben-Hadad's army with blindness: even though they worshipped idols all their lives. When Elisha asked Yahweh to strike them with blindness Yahweh obliged him in order that he would not be captured.

Elisha told Ben-Hadad's men; "This is not the road and this is not the city. Follow me, and I will lead you to the man you are looking for." And he led them to Samaria.

After they entered the city of Samaria, Elisha prayed; "Yahweh, open the eyes of these men so they can see." Then Yahweh opened their eyes and they looked, and there they were, inside Samaria.

When Jehoram, the king of Israel saw them, he asked Elisha; "Shall I kill them, Elisha? Shall I kill them?"

"No, do not kill them!" he replied; "Did you take them captive with your sword and bow? Would you slay those you capture: is it really your custom to kill those whom you bring into captivity? No. So set food and water before them so that they may eat and drink and then go and return to their master."

So Jehoram prepared a great feast for them, and after they had finished eating and drinking, he sent them away, and they returned to their master. So the bands from Aram stopped raiding Israel's territory. Though the kindness of Elisha and the king of Israel changed the hearts of these raiders, it did not change the heart of Ben-Hadad, the king of Aram. Some time later, he mobilized his entire army and the Arameans assembled all of their troops: launching a large and unprecedented full-scale attack on northern Israel against Jehoram. They marched up and laid siege to Samaria and besieged Jehoram in the securely walled city. With the city thus surrounded, all business and trade were prevented from entering or leaving, and the plan was to eventually starve the population into surrender.

> When Hannibal besieged Casiline, one mouse was sold for two hundred pence. At the siege of Scodra puddings made of dogs' guts were dearly bought.

There was a great famine in the city of Samaria for the siege strategy successfully starved them. The famine was so bad and lasted so long that a donkey's head sold for eighty shekels of silver, and a quarter of a cab of pigeon dung for five shekels: pigeon dung may be hotter than ordinary dung, but in other respects it might be fitter for nourishment as it is made of the best and purest grains and has some moisture in it. That is to say they became so expensive that only the rich could afford them: five shekels were more than a labourer's monthly wage.

As the king of Israel was walking along the wall, a woman, standing with another he passed by, cried out to him; "Help me, my lord the king!" He assumed that the cry of the woman was her asking for food.

"Don't ask me," he replied. "Let Yahweh help you! If Yahweh does not help you, where could I get help for you, from the threshing floor or from the winepress?" Her manner though indicated that the help she requested of him was not in relation to food. He therefore paused and proceeded to inquire what it was she wanted of him. Jehoram asked her; "What's the matter, what is troubling you?"

The woman answered; "That woman," she said pointing to the woman standing nearby; said to me, 'Give up your son and we will eat him today; and tomorrow we'll eat my son.' And so we reached an agreement that first one should be eaten, and then the other: that we should feed upon one as long as it would last, and then on the other; for our agreement is not limited precisely to a day and tomorrow. So we cooked my son. We boiled him and ate him up. The next day I said to her; 'Give up your son so that we may eat him,' but she had hidden him. He may even already be dead, and she's hid him that she might eat him alone without me!" When the king heard what the woman said, he rent his robes; and as he walked along the wall trying to process what he had heard, the people looked up and they could see that underneath his robes he was wearing sackcloth on his body (an important person is permitted to gird themselves in sackcloth as a sign of mourning and to pray for mercy only if they are certain their prayer will be answered).

Jehoram remembered that Moses had foretold of such an evil coming should the people turn away from Yahweh: that if they did enemies would besiege them at their gates until their high and fortified walls, in which they had put their trust, came down throughout all the land: which Yahweh had given them. And at that time they would; eat the fruit of your own womb, the flesh of your sons and your daughters whom Yahweh your God has given you'.

Jehoram said; "May God deal with me, be it ever so severely, if the head of Elisha son of Shaphat remains on his shoulders today!"

At this point in time Elisha was sitting in his house, and the elders were sitting with him. The king sent a messenger

> 'But if despite this you will not listen to me and you walk away from me, then I will walk away from you in fury. I myself will punish you seven times over for your sins. Then you will eat the flesh of your sons and the flesh of your daughters. I will destroy your high places; cut down your incense altars, and heap your lifeless bodies on the lifeless remains of your idols; and my soul will despise you.'
> Leviticus 26:27-30

ahead, but before the messenger arrived, Elisha said to the elders; "Do you see! This murderer is sending someone to cut off my head. Watch and when the messenger comes, shut the door and hold it barred fast against him. No doubt the sound of his master's footsteps will be following close behind him." While he was still talking to them, the messenger indeed came down to him followed soon thereafter by the King of Israel leaning on the arm of an officer. He said; "This calamity, this tradgedy, is from Yahweh. It is one of the curses that He cursed through Moses. What more can I hope and pray before Yahweh, why should I wait any longer for Yahweh to answer my prayers?"

Elisha replied; "Hear what Yahweh has said: This time tomorrow, a seah of the finest flour shall sell for a shekel at the gate of Samaria, and two seahs of barley for a shekel." The officer on whose arm the king was leaning spoke up and said to Elisha; "Even if Yahweh were to open the floodgates of the heavens, could this really happen?" Elisha retorted; "You shall see it with your own eyes!"

And so it came to pass that Yahweh caused the Arameans to hear the sound of chariots, horses, and a great army, so that they quailed; "The king of Israel has hired the Hittite and Egyptian kings to attack us!" So they got up and fled in the dusk; abandoning their tents, horses and donkeys. They left the camp as it was and ran for their lives. So on the morrow the people went out of Samaria and plundered the camp of the Arameans. So a seah of the finest flour indeed sold for a shekel, and two seahs of barley sold for a shekel, as Yahweh had said.

QUESTIONS TO PONDER

- When reflecting on what you know of wartime stories, I wonder what questions the story raises for you.

- I wonder how do you react towards the treatment of the children.

- I wonder how do you react towards the responses of the two women.

- Reviewing how the different characters behave, what tools of manipulation and abuse can you see?

- Where in this story do you see trauma, and what are its effects?

- I wonder what in this story unsettles you the most.

- I wonder how we can minister to people who have experienced the types of trauma identifiable in this story.

WAR

Elisha the prophet arrived in Damascus at a time when Ben-Hadad, the king of Aram, was ill. His illness was the result of the disgrace and discredit into which he had fallen since his army fled from before the walls of Samaria. The king was told; "Elisha, the servant of Yahweh, is on his way here." Ben-Hadad said to Hazael (which means God has seen), his court official; "Take a gift with you and go to meet Elisha. Ask him to speak to Yahweh and inquire of Yahweh: Will I recover from this illness?"

> Hazael was not a member of the royal family. Assyrian records called Hazael the 'son of a nobody' (a usurper) and his lineage was not recorded because he was a commoner.

So Hazael went to meet Elisha. He took with him, as a gift, forty camel-loads of all the bounty of Damascus. As Damascus was a trade centre between Egypt, Asia Minor, and Mesopotamia it had within it the finest merchandise of the ancient Near East. Ben-hadad gave such an impressive gift believing it would influence Elisha's prediction.

Hazael came and stood before Elisha and asked; "Your son, King Ben-hadad of Aram, has sent me to you to ask: Will I recover from this illness?"

Elisha said to him; "Go and say to him, 'You will recover.' However, Yahweh has revealed to me that he will die." By this Elisha meant that Ben-Hadad would not die of his current illness, but rather that he would die by assassination. Elisha fixed his gaze steadily on him and kept his face expressionless for a long time until Hazael became uncomfortable. Elisha held in his expression of grief, for he wanted to cry; he held it in, so that he would not cry in front of Hazael. He made a concentrated effort to stand and control himself, but as Hazael was not leaving, and the grief so overwhelming, Elisha began to weep.

Hazael saw Elisha start crying and asked; "For what reason does my sovereign lord weep?"

Elisha looked at him and replied; "Because I know," he paused with a sniff, "I weep because I know the harm and the evil you will do to the Israelite people. I see that you will send people out to set fire to the fortified cites of the Israelites. Their

> Menahem, after becoming king of Israel, invaded Tiphsah (and its territory), to punish them for not supporting him. Because it did not surrender, Menahem massacred its people and ripped open all its pregnant women. 2 Kings 15:16

little ones will be dashed to pieces before their eyes. Their houses will be looted, and their wives will be raped. I see that you will smite with deadly intent and kill their young men with the sword and their bowels will be split. I know that you will dash their little suckling children to pieces against the walls and the ground. And I know that you will rip open their pregnant women in order to expose their foetus."

"But how," asked Hazael; *"But what is your servant, who is a mere dog, that he should perform such a great and mighty thing?"*

In times of war, kings use different techniques to achieve victory against their enemies. They develop policies of uncontrolled violence, intimidation, and terror, in order to force their enemies into submission. Soldiers under them will cast aside their sense of humanity. No decent person likes war, but war is a reality in a world where

human beings lust after power and control. Hazael was not a decent man and took delight in cruelty and evil. That is why he saw Elisha's vision as a great and mighty thing.

Elisha replied; "Yahweh has shown me a vision of you as king of Aram." Indeed, before Elijah ascended into the heavens, Yahweh had told him to anoint Hazael as king of Aram. Yet it had been a long time before the *opportunity arose for Hazael to be king. But from that time he had sought an opportunity to betray Ben-Hadad. He used to lie and devise mischief and iniquity upon his bed; he had himself in a way that is not good; and he abhorred not evil.*

So Hazael left Elisha and returned to Damascus and went before his king and master. Ben-Hadad then asked him; "Tell me, did anything happen? Did Elisha receive you? What did Elisha say to you?" Hazael replied; "Yes, Elisha received me, and he told me that you would recover from this illness."

That night Hazael lay down and worked evil upon his bed: intending to put these plans into practice early in the morning. The next day Hazael took a thick, netted cloth, dipped it in water and spread it over the king's face He told Ben-Hadad that he was doing this to give him some relief from his illness. However, he actually intended to kill him! Hazael smothered him and so Ben-Hadad died. Then Hazael succeeded him as king and reigned in his place.

In the fifth year of King Joram son of Ahab of Israel—Jehoshaphat had been king of Judah— Jehoram, son of King Jehoshaphat of Judah became king. He was thirty-two years old when he became king, and he reigned in Jerusalem eight years.

Jehoram walked in the ways of the kings of Israel, just as the house of Ahab had done. He married a daughter of Ahab and did evil in Yahweh's eyes. Yet on account of King David, Yahweh was unwilling to destroy Judah: for Yahweh had promised David that when his days were fulfilled and he rested with his fathers, Yahweh would maintain a lamp for David, raising up offspring after him, and establish his kingdom forever.

During his reign, the Edomites rebelled against Judah's rule and set up a king of their own. Jehoram slept with his fathers and was buried with his fathers in the City of David. His son Ahaziah succeeded him as king.

In those days Yahweh began to reduce Israel; and Hazael harassed, abused and oppressed them throughout the territory of Israel.

QUESTIONS TO PONDER

- When reflecting on your experiences of politics and political ambition, I wonder what questions this story raises for you.

- I wonder how do you react towards Hazael.

- I wonder how do you react towards the response of Elisha.

- Reviewing how the different characters behave, what tools of manipulation and abuse can you see?

- Where in this story do you see trauma, and what are its effects?

- I wonder what in this story unsettles you the most.

- I wonder how we can minister to people who have experienced the types of trauma identifiable in this story.

www.ingramcontent.com/pod-product-compliance
Lightning Source LLC
Chambersburg PA
CBHW070524100426
42743CB00010B/1942